☝ **W9-BDW-974**

E. B. WHITE
Some Writer!
~~~❦~~~

For some time Andy had been thinking about writing another children's story. He knew he wanted to write about the animals in his barn and he definitely wanted to save a pig's life. He had not forgotten how upset he felt when his pig died, how the experience had frightened him. He had found it puzzling that he should fight for the life of a creature that he was raising to kill and eventually eat. It was this puzzle he wanted to explore.

One day Andy was passing through the shed and happened to look up. There was a large gray spider spinning an egg sac. He stopped to watch her as she wound her delicate white line round and round, up and around the eggs she had laid. Leaving for New York a few days later, Andy decided to take the egg sac with him. He found a box, made air holes in the top, and gently placed the sac inside. After a few weeks, he noticed tiny spiders coming out of the holes in the box and spinning delicate lines all over the objects on his dresser. Andy was thrilled.

He did not know very much about spiders, but now he wanted to learn all about them. In the library he found books that described everything about spiders' habits: what they ate, where they lived, how many kinds there were. Andy was going to call his spider Charlotte.

E. B. White with Minnie, at his New Yorker *office*

E.B. WHITE
Some Writer!

A Biography by
BEVERLY GHERMAN

ILLUSTRATED WITH PHOTOGRAPHS

A Beech Tree Paperback Book • New York

All photographs courtesy, The E. B. White Collection, Department of Rare Books, Cornell University Library, except for pages 24 and 58, courtesy of Charles R. Gherman.

All photographs courtesy of the E. B. White Collection,
Department of Rare Books, Cornell University Library,
except for pages 24 and 58 that are courtesy of Charles R. Gherman.
Copyright © 1992 by Beverly Gherman.
All rights reserved. No part of this book may be reproduced or
utilized in any form or by any means, electronic or mechanical,
including photocopying, recording or by any information storage
and retrieval system, without permission in writing from
Atheneum, a division of Macmillan Publishing Company,
866 Third Avenue, New York, NY 10022.
Printed in the United States of America.
First edition published in 1992 by Atheneum.
First Beech Tree Edition, 1994. Published by arrangement with Atheneum.

Library of Congress Cataloging-in-Publication Data

Gherman, Beverly.
E. B. White : some writer! / by Beverly Gherman.
p.   cm.
Originally published: New York : Atheneum, 1992.
Includes bibliographical references and index.
ISBN 0-688-12826-2
1. White, E. B. (Elwyn Brooks), 1899–   —Biography—Juvenile literature.
2. Authors, American—20th century—Biography—Juvenile literature.
[1. White, E. B. (Elwyn Brooks), 1899–
2. Authors, American.]   I. Title.
[PS3545.H5187Z66   1994]
818'.5209—dc20   [B]   93-35962   CIP   AC

For Cindy, who gave me the inspiration

All that I hope to say in books,
all that I ever hope to say,
is that I love the world.
— E. B. WHITE

ACKNOWLEDGMENTS

I am grateful to E. B. White's family, Joel and Allene White and Roger Angell, for sharing their memories with me; to Nancy Angell Stableford and Martha White for their warm letters to Andy; to Stan Waterman and Jerome Weidman for their recollections; to Lucy Burgess, at Cornell's Olin Library, who provided me with the material and photographs I needed from the White Collection.

My thanks to Scott Elledge for his detailed biography, to Dorothy Lobrano Guth for her book of letters, and to E. B. White's own books, which continue to bring pleasure with every reading.

CONTENTS

1

A LUCKY MAN

*W*henever E. B. White was asked to accept an award for one of his books, he found an excuse for not attending the ceremony. In 1970, when *Charlotte's Web* won the Claremont Center's Award, he sent them a speech describing how Wilbur fainted with excitement after he won his special prize at the fair. It took a bite from Templeton the rat to revive him. White said he would faint just as Wilbur had if he were forced to stand up before the audience and read his own speech. But he thanked them for liking *Charlotte* and said he felt "very lucky to have gained the ear of children. . . ."

White received mail from his fans all the time. One child sent him a letter addressed to the father of *Charlotte's Web*.

He was also the father of *Stuart Little* and *The Trumpet of the Swan*. But he did not spend his life writing for children. He waited until he was forty-five to write his first children's book, *Stuart*, and he was almost seventy when he wrote his third and last children's book, *Trumpet*. Before, during, and after, he penned essays, poems, and short stories for adults.

He never wrote down to children, nor did he feel he had to plan happy endings for them. In his adult essays, he said what he thought was important and didn't worry about offending people. He liked a little touch of magic and fantasy in his life and in his stories, no matter who might read them.

As a writer, he never sat still for long. He had to get out in the world. He fueled his writing with the events in his life, with the wonders of nature on his farm or at the zoo, and with his strong sense of right and wrong.

When he was a young man he wanted to travel far and wide. After graduating from college in 1922, he drove a Model T Ford across the country and took a ship up to Alaska, savoring the sights and sounds of people and places. He described everything in his journal as he had been doing since he was a boy. Many of his early verses were published. Later, most of his sketches from those years were also published.

In 1925 White submitted his work to a brand-new magazine—the *New Yorker*—and for the next fifty years he was associated with the magazine in one way or another. He also wrote for other magazines, always complaining that he didn't like having to meet deadlines. Sometimes he insisted he preferred to be out sailing, or feeding his geese, hens, and sheep. But he discovered he had to keep writing too. It was a habit he had started when he was an eight-year-old boy and he could not shake it.

He found life in New York City stimulating, but he also loved living on a saltwater farm in Maine, where he could go sailing when he was through with all his chores. His writing reflects these contrasts of city and country: thoughtfulness, sadness, and humor; his need to be alone, as well as to have close companionship. A *New Yorker* colleague wrote that his words were "so plain and so clearly pleasurable—a glass of cool water, a breeze on one's face—that they did not feel like literature."

He took complicated ideas and made them seem simple. He didn't mind sharing his innermost thoughts with his readers. To one reader he confessed that writing was "hard work for me and usually not attended with any joy. It has its satisfactions but the act of writing is often a pure headache.... When I want some fun, I don't write, I go sailing."

When people tried to label him a humorist, he objected. He felt he observed the world, sometimes with humor, sometimes with pleasure, often with criticism. He recognized the thin line between laughter and tears in his own life and when he went out to look at other people's lives. In his sketch about a man trying to find a job, we may be chuckling as the man reads job lists and White intersperses popular song lyrics, but we're also moved because the man is hungry and needs to find work.

Born in the seventh month, on the eleventh day—a lucky combination—White always thought of himself as a lucky man. He felt lucky when his work was published, when he fell in love and married Katharine, when his son, Joel, was born, whenever he witnessed the hatching of goslings, or when he received an award for one of his books. He felt especially lucky that children liked his books.

By his eighties he had given up ice skating, but he still went canoeing and bike riding. One day as he pedaled along the road on his old three-speed bicycle he noticed a coyote following behind him. White kept moving at a good pace. The coyote did, too. After a time White decided the animal meant him no harm. He was only curious to know what kept the ancient, white-haired man going.

2

MOUNT VERNON
BOYHOOD

*E*very morning the children of Public School 2 assembled in a large room to salute the flag and listen to the principal read a passage from the Bible. Afterward a student was asked to stand and recite. Elwyn "suffered tortures every day of the school year," worrying that he would be called. It didn't matter that his last name began with *W* and was at the end of the alphabet. He still worried. And one day his worst fears were realized. They had come to the *W*s. It was Elwyn's turn to step up on the platform. It was even worse than he imagined. His voice failed him, his knees shook, and his heart raced. He thought he would die.

By the time Elwyn reached the fifth grade, his fear of public speaking had grown along with him. Yet no matter

Elwyn with his older brothers, Stanley and Albert, 1906

how much he protested, his teacher would not excuse him from reciting a poem as all students were expected to do. Facing the audience of teachers and students, Elwyn could not control his tongue. Instead of saying, "Footprints on the sands of time," as Longfellow had written the line, out came, "Footprints on the tands of sime." He might have been able to complete the last stanzas of the poem if he had not heard

Mount Vernon home in which Elwyn was born

giggling in the audience. That caused him to forget everything. All he wanted to do was jump off the platform and hide. Elwyn was certain he would never be dragged on a platform again. And he wasn't. Throughout his life he continued to refuse requests to appear for awards and honors. He might write a speech to be read by someone else, but he was taking no chances on giving the speech himself.

A family portrait when Elwyn was a baby, 1900

The Summit Avenue home where Elwyn Brooks White was born on July 11, 1899, was a large, comfortable house in Mount Vernon, New York. Only a short train ride away from bustling New York City, it seemed like another world. The two places were opposites in every way. Mount Vernon was a rural community filled with lovely houses, tree-lined streets, and handsome gardens. In New York City most people worked in tall office buildings and lived in tall apartment buildings.

Elwyn enjoyed riding his bike, skating, and sledding in rural Mount Vernon, yet he was close enough to visit New York City, where he could watch parades as they passed in front of his father's workplace, the Horace Waters Piano Company on Fifth Avenue.

Both of Elwyn's parents were born in Brooklyn, New York, and both of them had quit school with only a grammar school education. Elwyn was the last of their six children, born when his parents were in their forties. He had three older sisters and two brothers.

His father, Samuel, left school at thirteen to work as an errand boy for the Waters Piano Company. Eventually he became president of the company, which prospered until 1929, when the depression caused it and many other businesses to fail. In those years many people lost their jobs and could not afford housing and food for their families. Pianos were one of the many luxuries they had to give up.

Elwyn's mother, Jessie, was a warmhearted woman who encouraged her children to study and get good educations even though she had been unable to complete her own. Her three sons graduated from Cornell and one daughter, Lillian, graduated from Vassar. Throughout her life Jessie wrote long letters to her children, keeping them all informed about one another. To Elwyn she passed on her love of flowers and tenderness toward animals, especially newborn creatures.

Jessie's father was William Hart, a well-known landscape artist, and the White home was filled with art and music, even though guests were rarely invited. Elwyn said later that he hadn't even known what a dinner party was until he was eighteen and had gone away from home. Instead of guests, the parlor was filled with musical instruments, and each of the children played at least one. Surrounding the grand piano were violins, drums, guitars, a mandolin, and a cello. Elwyn took lessons on the piano and cello and mastered the mandolin. He also loved to compose his own music. He and his older brother Stanley often played duets together. Sometimes they changed the music's tempo to suit themselves, racing through passages of a Beethoven sonata with abandon.

Samuel loved nature and travel. He also loved words and would always send the children to look up unfamiliar words in their big *Webster's Unabridged Dictionary* in Albert's room. He was also known for the amusing limericks he created for the family.

Elwyn liked to use the *Webster's* but sometimes found it frustrating. One day he waited until no one was looking and sneaked into Albert's room to search for the word *doylee* because he was convinced it was a dirty word. Finally, a few years later, he learned that a doily was merely a decorative cloth like the one his mother used on a plate of cookies.

By first grade Elwyn could read, because brother Stanley had taught him to sound out the words in articles from the *New York Times*. This did not make Elwyn very popular with the other children, nor with Miss Hackett, his teacher. But Stanley, who was eight years older, continued to teach his younger brother everything he could. After working on reading, he gave Elwyn instruction in physics and canoeing, and in practical matters such as how to trim the fingernails on one's right hand, and how to use a jackknife.

Elwyn kept his own room tidy and loved to lie in bed listening to the outdoor sounds of neighbor children playing, birds singing, and the milkman delivering bottles of milk. Once when he was home sick in bed, nine-year-old Elwyn wrote to his brothers, who were both attending Cornell University, telling them he would be going to Cornell too in about eight more years. In the same letter, he also reported

Elwyn with his dog, in front of the house

the news that a neighbor child had died without medical care and that he had a new book of piano music.

His letters to his brothers were signed differently every time. Sometimes he used a formal "Master Elwyn Brooks White"; sometimes, he signed with a casual "En." At other times he used code names or called himself "Buttercup."

A story of a little mouse.

Once there was a wise little mouse,
At least that's what he thought,
But this experience shows you
Just what his wisdom brought.

One day as he walked through the kitchen,
A wire too he spied,
And hanging by was a crumb of cheese
Which he very carefully eyed.

Then he decided he'd leave some
So in the box he stepped,
Farther and farther and farther
Very cautiously he crept.

But all of a sudden the trap sprung
And cut right off his head,
For the cruel trap had been laid for him
And there he lay quite dead.

As a lesson for a little mouse
I certainly call it wise,
That mice had better be careful,

Elwyn's poem "A story of a little mouse"

He sent Albert a poem he had written about a mouse, and a few months later that poem won a prize in *Woman's Home Companion*. Then he wrote that he had made friends with a mouse and built him a gymnasium and taught him tricks. His fascination with small creatures would last throughout his life. Stuart Little was not yet in his thoughts, but Elwyn was storing up information about this relative of Stuart's for the future.

There was always a dog in Elwyn's life. His first dog, Mac, a collie, was not allowed to live in the house, which made Elwyn very sad until he built Mac an elaborate sheepskin-lined house to be kept in the barn. Later he wrote that for six years Mac "met me at the same place after school and conveyed me home—a service he thought up himself."

Elwyn loved all kinds of animals. He raised pigeons, canaries, lizards, and turtles. He studied them, standing quietly, content to learn by observation. This kind of patience taught him more than any book. He especially envied the boy down the street because Kenny had elaborate cages for his animals and owned a monkey and a raccoon.

Behind the White home was a stable for the horses with quarters for the coachman who tended them. One day, Elwyn's father brought fifty eggs and an incubator to the stable. Still not very tall, Elwyn had to stretch to see the eggs warming in the long tray. The coachman pointed out the slight cracks in the eggs where chicks were just beginning to struggle out of their shells, and the boy heard soft peeps coming from the back of the tray. Standing on tiptoe, he saw one tiny beak! Then there were two more! Soon, damp yellow chicks were hatching everywhere, and Elwyn himself was ready to burst with excitement.

When he was eight, Elwyn began writing daily in a diary. To make it sound more important, he called it his journal. He didn't waste words on what he had eaten for dinner or studied at school that day. Instead he began asking himself difficult questions about life and about his relationships with his parents and his friends. He wrote about his fears of the dark cellar and the damp lavatory in the school basement. He told about his shyness toward girls. If he could not speak out, at least he could put his thoughts on paper.

3

GROWING UP

N ot only did Elwyn write in his journal and send letters to his brothers; he also wrote stories and poems and sent them off to the popular *St. Nicholas Magazine*. A friend told him the magazine tended to accept children's writing when it included kindness to animals. Eleven-year-old Elwyn submitted a dog story with that theme and won a silver medal for it. In it he described the forest:

All the trees wore a new fur coat, pure white, and the pines and evergreens were laden with pearl. Every living creature seemed happy. Squirrels frisked among the branches. . . . A few straggling quails were heard. . . .

All these harmless little wood creatures were noticed by Don [the dog] and he wanted to be after them, but I objected to harming God's innocent little folk when He had given the world such a bright, cheery morning to enjoy.

When he won a gold medal three years later, it was for an adventurous dog story, without the sticky sweetness of this earlier effort.

Elwyn worked hard while he was in school, studying arithmetic, geography, and spelling, but he was never much of a reader. The only books he liked were about animals or small boat voyages. Rather than read, he preferred to be outside biking and climbing trees. In the winter he loved ice skating, skiing, or playing hockey. His parents gave him unlimited freedom to explore. Their only rule was to be home in time for supper.

He was quite comfortable in the natural world except for his allergies. Elwyn had terrible hay fever, which gave him a stuffy nose and watery, itchy eyes. At night it was hard for him to breathe when he put his head down on the pillow. Usually at least one nostril was clogged and he had to breathe through the other one. Sometimes both nostrils were. Then he had to breathe through his mouth. He was afraid to close his eyes for fear he would forget to keep his mouth open.

His father thought Elwyn's hay fever would improve if the family spent the month of August at Great Pond, one of the Belgrade Lakes in Maine. From the time he was about six years old, this became the highlight of Elwyn's whole year. He could hardly wait for school to end so that he could plan and dream about going to Great Pond.

Getting to the lake took careful arranging. Samuel bought tickets on the Bar Harbor Express for the whole family, for their servant, and their dog. They left from New York's

Elwyn wearing high-button shoes, about 1910

Grand Central Station on the evening train, which arrived at Belgrade the next morning, over thirteen hours later. No matter how much the children teased her, Jessie always slept fully dressed in order to be ready for any emergency. They were met at the Belgrade station by a buckboard and team, which took everyone and everything the ten miles to Great Pond. No one seemed to mind that they lived in a rustic cabin and had to use an outhouse, or that meals were served at a nearby farmhouse.

For Elwyn, August at the lake meant happiness and good health. His hay fever was left behind. Each morning he was up with the sun, when the air was cool and silent. Stealthily, he set out in his green canoe to explore the creatures who lived along the shore. He watched turtles slide off wet logs, found nesting birds, heard croaking frogs, and saw the mist rise from the lake in the woods. He loved that quiet time alone.

But he also loved the noisier times when the whole family piled into a sixteen-foot motorboat Stan and Albert had made. They named it *Jessie*, after their mother, who didn't like the water at all, but was a good sport and joined everyone for trips to the general store across the lake. She sat clutching her parasol for shade, and perhaps for moral support. Elwyn too worried that the boat would sink because it was so crowded. When they reached shore, Samuel treated the family to the soft drink, Moxie, and bought a case of it to take back to the cabins. With the added weight, Elwyn worried even more that they would capsize, but they never did. Moxie was Samuel's favorite drink, and he insisted that it would continue to be more popular than that new Coca-Cola.

Elwyn canoeing at Belgrade Lakes, 1914

The month was always over too soon for Elwyn. Back he went to Mount Vernon and school. But August and the lake were never far from his thoughts and he knew he would be returning there summer after summer.

In high school, Elwyn envied the other boys who knew how to talk to girls, invite them to go to the drugstore for a soda, or even dance with them at school dances. He could do none of those things. He was terrible at small talk, he was too slight to become a football hero, he didn't like to smoke, and he didn't know how to dance. It seemed he had better stick to riding his bike in good weather or playing goalie in hockey games when the pond froze solid. Indoors, he played romantic music on the piano and composed poems about his dreams.

His sister Lillian, five years older and much wiser in social ways, tried to teach Elwyn how to behave with girls. She even invited him to join a group of her friends for an afternoon tea dance in New York. He went with them and discovered he could manage well enough to hold a conversation and maneuver a girl around the hotel dance floor.

Elwyn decided he was ready to repeat the outing now that he knew what to do. First, it meant getting up his courage to call a neighbor girl on the telephone. He kept going into the hall closet to use the wall phone and then going back to his room because he was too nervous. Finally he was able to ask the operator to ring the number.

Over and over he had rehearsed what he would say until it seemed simple: "Hello, Eileen, this is Elwyn White."

Instead, Eileen's mother answered. He could not adjust his greeting for Mrs. Thomas, and when Eileen came to the phone and said, "Hello, Elwyn," he repeated himself: "Hello, Eileen, this is Elwyn White." He was mortified, yet somehow he managed to propose his plan for the outing.

Eileen agreed to go with him to the tea dance at New York's Plaza Hotel. They took the train together but found little to say. It was easier to stare out the window or study the other passengers. Once in New York, Elwyn took her to the hotel, where they danced, drank tea, munched cinnamon toast, and then immediately took the train home. It was not a pleasant experience for either of them, as Elwyn remembered it. He had done everything by rote, unable to relax and enjoy being with Eileen. He hardly felt as if he had been in New York or out on a date.

At sixteen, Elwyn was much more comfortable skating in the moonlight on Siwanoy Pond with Mildred Hesse. Afterward he wrote a poem in his journal about the wonders of moonlight on the icy pond and a graceful young girl on his arm. He never spoke to Mildred during daylight. She existed only during "winter twilights, when the air grew still and the pond cracked and creaked under our skates. . . ."

In his senior year at Mount Vernon High School, he was assistant editor of the literary magazine, the *Oracle*, and two of his stories were published in it. That year he also wrote a strong letter to the editor of the *American Boy* objecting to an article about the trapping of fur-bearing animals for profit. He thought the magazine should have a more positive influence on its young readers. By now he was expressing a sincere concern about animal welfare, not trying to win medals. The editor was impressed with Elwyn's opinion and wrote to tell him.

The 1917 war in Europe seemed far away. Elwyn was busy studying Latin, ancient history, algebra, and biology. In his journal he was writing about his pigeons and about ice skating in the moonlight. At one point he wrote an editorial in the school paper urging the United States not to get involved in the European war.

As he read more about the war, Elwyn was no longer certain the United States should remain neutral. He began pasting articles about war issues in his journal and he also expressed how torn he felt. Sometimes he thought he should join the army. At other times he wanted to run off to France with the ambulance corps. Then he wondered about going to work on a farm for the war effort.

"I am living the life of a slacker, gorging my belly with food which others need," he told his journal on July 5, 1917. "I wish I were old enough to be drafted."

4

CORNELL

*E*lwyn graduated from high school in January 1917, with two scholarships for college, but he was not sure he should accept them. He kept weighing all his options and then realized he could not help the war effort at his age and that it would make sense for him to go on to college. After all, he had been dreaming about going to Cornell since he was eight years old, and every time he visited Stan and Albert there, he knew it was the right place for him. The handsome campus in Ithaca, New York, was set high on a hill, surrounded by trees and ponds and winding paths. He remembered how the trolley car ran up and down the hills between town and campus, and he could hardly wait to use it.

Once in Ithaca, he moved into a single dormitory room

Cornell University, 1990

overlooking Lake Cayuga. Although he was lonely and home-sick during the first few weeks of school, he gradually began to make friends and to get interested in his classes. Yet throughout his life he admitted he needed to be alone and private a great deal, whether he was on a busy campus or in a bustling city.

After several months he wrote in his journal, "I've been feeling sick for the past week and I think I must have consumption. If I have, I will leave college and travel for my health." Apparently his illness quickly passed, because he was also writing about his latest classes and about becoming a freshman reporter on the *Cornell Daily Sun*. He spent more time and energy on the paper than he did in any of his courses, but he still managed to get by.

The school year ended early so that students could find work in war industries. Elwyn again debated about all the things he should do and finally went to work for his father in the credit department at the Waters Piano Company. All summer he worried about whether he should go back to school or go to war. He was now eighteen, old enough to enlist, and yet not sure he wanted to fight.

When he went back to school in September 1918, he registered for the draft with most of the other young men. Shortly after that he enlisted in the Student Army Training Corps, which meant he would have to drill and study military subjects along with his regular courses. The war ended in November 1918, and Elwyn was out of service a month later. The main thing he remembered about being a soldier was that many of the new recruits were sick with the flu. To avoid getting sick, he bought an ample supply of licorice drops because he had been told they would prevent the illness.

At the beginning of 1919, classes at Cornell were back to normal. By then Elwyn had been given a new name. Because the first president of the university was Andrew White, his friends decided he should be the next Andrew White—Andy, for short. The name stuck. After that, he was Andy most of the time. Often he still signed himself "En" when he wrote to the family, but Andy seemed to suit him best of all.

At first Andy did not want to join a fraternity, worrying that he was not the type. Again his sister Lillian had to give him advice. She assured him that it would be good for him to belong to a fraternity but that he should not call it a "frat." That's "small-town stuff," she reminded him. She also told him to stop taking only cold showers because they were not getting him clean. He needed a good hot scrub. He listened to his sister about showers and fraternities. When he joined Phi Gamma Delta, he discovered that several of the other members also wrote for the paper, so he fit right in. By his junior year he was elected president.

Andy wrote articles, poems, and one-liners for Cornell's paper, the *Daily Sun*, and was named editor in chief in his junior year. In those years the *Sun* was the only morning paper in Ithaca, which meant that the community as well as the students read it. Writing for the paper gave Andy great exposure and a real sense of responsibility. He wrote editorials about social issues, objecting when he saw prejudice or mistaken idealism. He thought a teacher should not be dismissed because she belonged to the Communist party. The test, he said, was how good a teacher she was. He thought it was terrible that a track meet had been canceled because black students were not welcome on a southern campus.

He sometimes reprinted a headline or news item and then added his own witty comment. These became the form he later used for newsbreaks in the *New Yorker* magazine. One of his editorials won first prize at a convention of college newspapers. In it he lamented that many students seemed unable to express themselves on paper.

Andy spent most of his evenings getting out the paper. Since the trolley stopped running by eleven, he had to walk up the hill from the downtown *Sun* offices in the early hours of the morning. Taking a shortcut through the cemetery, he didn't dawdle, but he appreciated the peace and quiet around him after the excitement of the noisy presses and the rush to meet deadlines.

He found time to attend Monday night gatherings at the

home of Professor Bristow Adams, where they ate cookies and drank cocoa and where the conversation was always stimulating. Professor Adams taught journalism and knew how important it was to give students a chance to express their ideas about world affairs, personal affairs, or whatever they wanted to bring up. Andy became close friends with Professor Adams and his wife, and often visited at other times, to talk or play the piano while Mrs. Adams sang.

Once a month, on Saturday evenings, Professor Martin Sampson opened his home to the Manuscript Club. Andy was a regular there with his latest poem or essay, and always had comments to share about work the other students brought. Professor Sampson read everyone's work aloud with a great sense of style and drama. He especially encouraged Andy to continue writing because he liked his humor and his satire. Afterward the group munched on cheese and crackers and sipped ginger beer.

Years later, Andy said he majored in English because he "didn't know what else to do, but mostly because [he] did have a strong tendency to write." He always insisted he didn't have a good literary background and that he had not retained most of the material he was supposed to have learned in the other classes he took.

English 8 was a different story. Taught by Professor William Strunk, who also came to the Manuscript Club, it was an advanced writing course that gave Andy specific guidelines for writing well. Strunk had very definite ideas about how students should express themselves and had written a book for them which he called the "little book." He told them to write simple, direct sentences. He insisted they use correct grammar. Because his most important rule was to "Omit needless words," Andy described him as "Sergeant Strunk snapping orders to his platoon."

One other professor who influenced him for life was George Lincoln Burr, who taught medieval history. From Professor Burr he learned what it meant to live in a free society, even though he couldn't keep all the details of medieval history in his head. In college and for the rest of his life, whenever he found individual freedom being threatened, Andy had to speak up.

By his last year at Cornell, Andy found he could talk to girls. He had even fallen in love with one, although he had not been able to tell her that. Alice Burchfield was a junior and he not only talked to her and walked with her under the stars, he began writing poems about her. At least on paper Andy was no longer the tongue-tied, shy Elwyn he had been when he left high school. He was on the way to becoming E. B. White and already had signed a letter with this strong name. He was a competent editor and journalist, well respected by the other students; he had been asked to join honorary societies; and now he had a girlfriend too.

In the 1921 yearbook, the *Cornellian*, Andy had five lines of credit under his name because he had participated in so many activities during his years at Cornell. It was one of the longest entries in the yearbook. But all too soon it was graduation time and his wonderful college years were coming to an end. Now he had to find a job. He was offered a teaching position at the University of Minnesota, but as much as he admired his professors, he knew he could not stand up before a classroom of students. The platform at Public School 2 was still too vivid a memory.

─── 5 ───

GOING WEST

*A*ndy knew he couldn't teach, but he thought he could become a good journalist. After graduation, one day in the fall of 1921, he took an early train from Mount Vernon into New York City with high hopes of finding a newspaper job.

All that day, and for days afterward, he met managing editors, until he felt as though he had spoken to every managing editor of every newspaper in New York City. Each one told him the same thing—Sorry, there are no openings—and sent him on to another editor who might need him.

The noise of the presses, the smell of the ink, the hectic activity inside those pressrooms, all made him nostalgic for the *Sun* room, where he had spent so much of his life at

Cornell. Once again he wanted to be part of a newspaper. He wanted to write important editorials and to have an influence on his readers. The New York editors were not impressed.

Finally he found a job with the United Press located right in the newspaper district on Park Row. He was to edit copy as it raced over the ticker tape and send it out to newspapers in other cities. Many of the bulletins were sports stories listing scores of football and baseball games. One day he counted 1,270 bulletins he had handled in less than three hours. It kept him busy and meant that he did not return to Mount Vernon until late in the evening, but he never seemed too tired to write once he was back in his old bedroom. There he poured out his thoughts in his journal, wrote pensive poems and stories and long letters to Alice.

By November he found a new job writing ads for a public relations firm. Then in January 1922 he began writing publicity for the News Service of the American Legion. The job still didn't excite him. But getting his poems published certainly did. Every few days he found one in the "Conning Tower" and "The Bowling Green," newspaper columns by important New York writers of the day.

In his journal he described the "excitement of finishing a love poem long after midnight, then carrying it out into the cold streets to drop it in a letter box at the corner. Two mornings later, I would be up early to buy a paper, hot off the presses, and find my immortal verse enshrined. . . ." He was never paid a penny for his words, but that didn't matter to Andy. He was writing for "the pure love of it, and the glory."

His Cornell friend Howard Cushman came to New York

to visit Andy in February. They had often talked about taking a trip together and now they decided it was a perfect time to travel west. Andy had recently bought a Model T Ford he named Hotspur, the Swift, for the warrior in Shakespeare's *Henry IV*. He felt there was nothing to keep him in New York. His job was certainly not challenging. Why didn't he and Howard get their belongings together and go? Afterward he explained, "I did *my* dropping out after I graduated."

They packed Hotspur with their two Corona typewriters, clothes, cooking equipment, a fiddle and a mouth organ, plenty of books and writing paper, and of course a dictionary. Once they were ready to go, Andy announced his plans to his startled parents. He had not said a word to them earlier for fear they would not understand or would try to prevent him from going. But they must have trusted his judgment, since they made no attempt to talk him out of the trip.

Leaving Mount Vernon on the afternoon of March 9, they planned to make their first stop at Cornell. Andy was eager to get there because he wanted to discuss some important things with Alice, who was completing her last year at the university. During the trip he kept thinking about the romantic moments they had spent together looking at the stars and walking around campus holding hands. He thought it might be time to tell Alice how he felt about her.

They arrived on Saturday night just in time to join old friends at the Manuscript Club and then to participate in Professor Adams's Monday night open house. Andy thought about Alice, but made no effort to contact her until their last morning on campus. Then he raced over to the bridge where he expected Alice to cross on her way to class. He paced back and forth waiting for her. Somehow it didn't occur to him

Cushman in Model T, summer 1922

that she had no idea he was going to be there, that he had not even told her about his trip. He was not used to planning ahead or sharing his plans with someone else. She never did show up that day. Several weeks later he and Cush made their way to her home in Buffalo when Alice was there for spring vacation, and Andy met with her at last.

To her great surprise, he asked her to marry him. The hesitant way he spoke and the way he had avoided her at Cornell made her believe he did not really mean it. They agreed to remain friends and correspond while he was away.

For Andy it was easier to write about his feelings than to express them to Alice in person. After he left her he wrote, "I suppose you wonder why I don't act like a normal person. I wonder too. . . . I used to write things about you and not show them to you because such a thing as marriage seemed a thousand years away and I didn't think it was fair [to] say things promiscuously." He was not ready to settle down to a job or to the responsibility of marriage at that time and Alice must have recognized his longing to be free and his need to explore the world.

Andy and Cush had not made specific plans for their trip. They would stop whenever something interested them, and would sell their experiences to newspapers along the way. As Andy wrote a friend, he and Cush were "jogging leisurely from one free meal to the next . . . writing a lot, selling a little. . . ."

In the 1920s people did not drive across the country the way they would in later years. Automobiles were still novelties, the connecting highway system had not yet been built, existing roads were in bad condition, and road signs didn't exist at all. Often the roads were so narrow that Hotspur had to back up and let another car pass.

They stopped in Louisville to see the Kenucky Derby horse race and at night found a grassy area for their sleeping bags. Just at dusk Andy heard his first whippoorwill repeatedly calling its own name, and he knew he would never forget the sound and the joy of sleeping under the stars.

A few days later Andy lost money on a race at Churchill Downs, but afterward he wrote a sonnet to the horse, jotting his ideas on an old paper napkin. That night, using the street light, he sat in Hotspur and typed out the final version of the poem. When he sold it to the *Louisville Herald*, he wrote Alice that his name—ELWYN BROOKS WHITE—was printed in such large type it even impressed him. He also decided this must be the only time a sonnet was written to recover losses from a horse race.

The following month he entered a limerick contest spon-

sored by the *Minneapolis Journal*, which printed the first four
lines and challenged its readers to complete the limerick:

> A young man who liked to rock boats
> In order to get people's goats
> Gave just one more rock
> Then suffered a shock

Andy searched for words to rhyme with goats. He filled
pages in his notebook looking for just the right line to submit
and finally he had it. A few days later he found his name—
E. B. White—now in small type—listed under the winning
entry:

> A bubble the spot now denotes.

In a long letter home, Andy told his family how proud
he was to be able to write a winning limerick in the tradition
of his father, the great limerick writer. And not only that, he
had won twenty-five dollars, which would come in very
handy.

When they ran out of winnings and couldn't sell an article
or poem, he and Cush had to find other ways to earn money.
Once, Andy wrote term papers for a fraternity brother. In
Minneapolis he sold roach powder, door to door. In Montana
he got a job playing the piano, while Cush harvested in the
hayfields. In Cody, Wyoming, he spent all day sanding an
open-air dance floor and made only three dollars. Later they
both picked fruit ten hours a day.

Near Walker, Minnesota, Andy fell and injured his elbow
when he jumped over a tent rope. There he was, on the
ground, with terrible pains shooting through his arm. He had

Andy, arm in sling, 1922

to drive himself to the hospital to get it x-rayed and was not released until the next day, with his arm in a sling. Not only was he in pain, but Cush was furious with him for hurting himself when he was alone. That was a lot of nerve, Cush told him. At least he could have waited until he had been there to help him.

Driving became more difficult now that he could use only one arm, especially when they had to make turns or park the car, but since Cush did not know how to drive at all, Andy had no choice. Cush continued to turn the crank to get the car started, and they moved on, despite Andy's throbbing elbow and his annoying hay fever. Nothing kept him from making friends with people they met along the way or enjoying the sights they found at Yellowstone and Glacier Park.

During a terrible rainstorm, he wrote Mrs. Adams that he was sitting in his pup tent typing a letter to her and imagining that he was in her home, "warm and full of cocoa. I even imagine that school children in unborn centuries will be taught to say, 'the poet White had a very good imagination.'" Andy had sold his typewriter in Cody for twenty dollars when they were short of money. Now he was using Cush's typewriter.

After spending time in Canada, they returned to the United States through the state of Washington, where Hotspur died just as they were heading up the steep ramp onto the Columbia River ferry. Andy lifted the hood and began searching for the problem. The ferry captain "leaned over the rail and stared," said Andy. "Then I saw that there was a hunger in his eyes that set him off from other men." He told them to push the car onto the ferry and he would study the problem with them as they crossed back and forth over the Columbia River. Andy described how the "skipper (who had once worked in a Ford garage) directed the amazing work of resetting the bones of my car." After eliminating everything else, the ferryman decided it was the main drive pinion.

Sure enough, when Andy replaced the part, Hotspur was ready to run and they were able to continue on their way.

Reporter White, Seattle, 1922

6

SEATTLE

*O*nce they arrived in Seattle in September, Andy decided he liked it there and would stay. He found a job as a reporter with the *Seattle Times*, which paid him forty dollars a week. He sold Hotspur and bought himself a small, sleek Ford coupé and a new typewriter, both on the installment plan.

Cush couldn't find a job and decided to go home, while Andy located a boardinghouse and moved in. Usually he didn't mind being alone, but the constant rain and gray skies of Seattle were hard to take. When Christmas came, it was especially difficult for him in his damp, dreary boardinghouse, even though he had put up holiday decorations in his room and his landlady had given him a new lamp. He tried to cheer himself by writing letters to his friends around the country.

Alice kept sending him gifts: a fountain pen when she heard he had lost his old one, ties he didn't like, handkerchiefs she stitched for him. She also continued to write regularly, while Andy found he was writing her less and less frequently.

At the newspaper, he quickly discovered he was not cut out to be a reporter. Covering murders made him ill; luncheon meetings were boring. He spent too much time composing and revising everything he wrote. At last his boss assigned him feature stories, which meant he would have more time to complete them. In March he was asked to write a daily column and he planned to include verse and comments on important events in the news. The column also gave him an opportunity to write about himself—to tell humorous stories, such as what happened to him when he went shopping for garters and found the number of color choices overwhelming. There should be only black garters available, he concluded, so that a man would not be forced to make decisions.

He continued to read the New York columnists Franklin Pierce Adams, who signed himself FPA, Don Marquis, and Christopher Morley, all of whom inspired him. He was also lucky to have a wise city editor, Mr. Johns, who gave him valuable advice when he was stuck writing a complicated story. Andy tried to tell the story from one angle, then he tried to tell it from another angle. He kept getting lost and felt unsure about how to proceed.

"Just say the words," Johns told him. And that made all the difference.

White went back to his desk and began to write, simply and clearly, explaining the facts as they had happened, and then adding his own details to make it a lively story. He realized that his editor had given him the same advice Professor Strunk had given him at Cornell. Be clear and simple in saying the words. It didn't make the writing easier. It was still hard work to get the story just right, but at least he had a guideline for how to do it.

Andy worked for the paper until June 1923, when there was a staff cut and he was dismissed. By then he had been in Seattle for about nine months and he still wanted to see Alaska before he went home. He bought himself a first-class ticket on the S. S. *Buford*, heading for Skagway, Alaska.

Halfway through the trip, he ran out of funds and begged the captain to give him a job. Andy became the night saloon-man, working from eight in the evening until six in the morning, preparing a late supper, serving it, and then cleaning up afterward. He loved being able to shock people who had known him previously as a passenger. One elderly woman was so startled seeing him in his white jacket, she remarked, "Goodness! How long have *you* been a waitress?"

As a passenger he had been able to dance and socialize with all the other passengers, but he felt he was missing something. Now that he was an employee, he became part of the inner workings of the ship, and it was exhilarating.

When his next job took him down to the firemen's mess at the bottom of the ship, he found still more challenges in getting along with the rugged men he served there. He knew he had to win the respect of these men and not let them know he had been a college student and a first-class passenger. He embellished the job experiences he'd had while crossing the country, saying he had been fired from each one. That quickly gained their respect. They knew he would be successful at this job when he managed to find them the extra oranges and dill pickles they craved, and to make whatever liquid concoctions they thought up. He learned to deal with their colorful language and the terrible heat of the mess, and to carry huge cauldrons of hot stew from the galley down a vertical ladder. Not only did he grew strong physically, but the farther down he went in the ship, the better he felt about himself.

Just before they were to dock in Seattle, a violent storm tossed the ship from side to side for three days. Most of the passengers became violently ill, but not Andy. He felt triumphant. He discovered that he could sway with the waves rather than try to resist them. "I reeled crazily through the corridors responding to the sea physically, as though the sea were a dancing partner whose lead I followed." Throughout his life he would continue to love—and fear—the sea's power.

He would look back on the Alaskan trip and his travels across the country as some of the most important experiences of his life. They showed him that he could handle any situation, on land and on sea, in fine weather or foul, and that he could be comfortable with people on any social level.

When the ship returned to Seattle, White left it and his job. He was ready to go home. He sold his car, packed his books and clothes, and bought a train ticket, just as his father had been urging him to do for some time. By then he had been away for eighteen months.

──7──

THE
NEW YORKER

*I*n September of 1923 Andy traveled back to New York on the Canadian Pacific Railroad. Sitting back as a passenger, he was able to enjoy the scenery in a way he had not at the wheel of Hotspur. Before going home, he planned to stop over in Buffalo to see Alice, who was still writing and sending him thoughtful gifts. He had not been as considerate. Sometimes he wrote only once a month, if that often.

When they were finally together, he told Alice about his Seattle job, about Alaska, about the many people he had met on his long odyssey across the country. He didn't talk about their future at all. Perhaps he knew he really was not ready to commit himself to marriage. He was only twenty-four and the time away had confirmed how important it was for him to be on his own. Also, he had no idea what he was planning to do with his life or even where he would find his next job. He left Alice without clarifying anything about their relationship.

In Mount Vernon he realized his parents were getting on in years. His father was sixty-nine and suffering from attacks of rheumatism. His mother was well and relieved to have him back. Andy was glad to see them, but it must have been difficult to live at home after being on his own for so long. Yet without any savings he could not pay rent elsewhere and it would take him time to build up those savings. He was going to have to make the best of it.

Once again Andy began reading the want ads, looking for a job. He found work in a New York advertising agency doing layout, which did not allow him to write. Instead he wrote in his journal and created poems and other humorous work at night in his boyhood bedroom. And when he wasn't writing he took his sixteen-foot canoe, which he had rigged with a sail, out on Long Island Sound to enjoy the glow of moonlight on the water.

In the spring of 1924 he wrote Alice saying that his feelings for her were always confused. Sometimes he thought of her as a good friend and at other times he thought he loved her, but now he had decided the relationship should end. He was sorry to have hurt her by his foolish ways. By then Alice might have been disappointed, but she could not have been very surprised. No matter what he said or wrote, his actions had always been the same. It was time for both of them to move forward with their lives.

A new magazine, the *New Yorker*, appeared on Thursday, February 19, 1925. Andy bought a copy for fifteen cents in

Grand Central Station on his way home to Mount Vernon and studied its cover. He saw a Regency dandy—later named Eustace Tilley—wearing a tall hat and a high collar, studying a butterfly through his monocle. Then he began to read the articles inside. There were short stories, verses, smart editorial comments, and reviews of New York art exhibits and musical events. He had heard that the editor, Harold Ross, was trying to appeal to sophisticated readers of New York, not little old ladies from the Midwest.

When a friend suggested that he submit his work to this new magazine, Andy thought he might just do it. Several months later he sent in a quirky piece on spring. It was accepted! Later an essay on the Bronx River was also published, and before long, many of his verses were included on *New Yorker* pages. Most of this early work expressed the joy he felt toward New York City. And now, at last, he was getting paid for writing it.

By the summer of 1925 Andy had saved enough money to move into a New York apartment in Greenwich Village with three Cornell friends. He also quit his job at the ad agency, planning to write and create on his own. His roommates left the house every morning bound for office jobs, while Andy stayed behind to clean up. After his chores were done he was supposed to sit down and write, but often he felt like wandering the city. Trips to the zoo or to the docks stimulated ideas for his writing, and once he could force himself back to the apartment, he found he had much to say about what he'd seen.

He realized he needed to find a part-time job to help pay his expenses and found one with another advertising agency, which paid him thirty dollars a week for writing copy about a new automobile. He continued to sell short pieces to the *New Yorker*, and in one story, "Child's Play," published in December of 1925, he found an original way to write about himself that others enjoyed. He discovered "the world would pay a man for setting down a simple, legible account of his own misfortunes."

In the story he told how a waitress spilled a glass of buttermilk on his blue suit and how he comforted the distressed young woman and then left her a generous tip, before making a grand exit from Child's Restaurant. Because the episode was written as a small play or vignette, and because he made fun of himself with gentleness, many readers identified with it.

In May he sent the *New Yorker* two sketches of men he had observed on his outings. Again he captured the sadness of their lives and coupled it with humor. Katharine Angell read the essays and suggested to her boss, Harold Ross, that they hire White to work on the magazine because she liked the pieces he kept sending them.

When Andy came to the office for a meeting, he was met by a very attractive Mrs. Angell. Her thick, dark hair pulled back into a bun, her large gray-green eyes set straight on him, she spoke to him with authority. Katharine Angell had started working on the magazine as a part-time manuscript reader but very quickly became a full-time editorial assistant, involved in every aspect of the publication, from art to fiction to the editorial columns. She knew literature well and had great skill in selecting and editing stories submitted to the magazine.

She took Andy to meet Harold Ross and the two of them

Andy with his friend James Thurber, 1929

offered him a job. Andy wasn't sure he wanted a job, he told
them. He liked being able to write on his own and send in
his work for publication, but he didn't think he could sit in
their offices and write. In fact, that June he left on a free trip
to Europe with only a day's notice. He needed to be able to
pick up and leave that way, just as he had done with Cush
when they impulsively decided to head west.

When he returned from Europe in August there were six
checks from the *New Yorker* awaiting him. As much as he
liked getting paid for what he wrote, he was still not sure he
wanted to take a steady job on the magazine. Ross and Angell
kept asking him to come to work, but he kept hesitating. In
January 1927, when he was twenty-seven years old, they finally
persuaded him to take a part-time job.

He would take the job, he told them, if he could continue
to travel around town and write about what he saw and about
what happened to him. One of the things Andy had learned
about himself was that he could not sit in an office for long
hours at a time and hope to produce good essays or poems.
He needed to be stimulated by what he saw and heard, by
what happened to him as he made his way through the day.

At first he shared a tiny office with James Thurber, and
the two men became close, admiring friends. They used to
inspire each other and even wrote a book together in 1929,
called *Is Sex Necessary?*, which was a spoof on all the sex
manuals being published in those days. Thurber doodled as
he wrote and then tossed the finished drawings on the floor
or into the wastebasket. Andy had been picking up all those
discards and from this collection, he selected many to illustrate
their book.

Thurber's zany line drawings of men and women, cats

and dogs, filled the pages, along with the wild and original theories the two thought up: Women make fudge to keep men at a distance. In turn, men began bringing candy to their lovers to keep them from making fudge.

The book brought both men attention they had not received previously. And Thurber's drawings no longer ended up in the trash. They became an important addition to the *New Yorker*.

White had done comments on news items when he was writing for the *Cornell Daily Sun*. He was good at thinking up just the right punch line when he saw an error of grammar or spelling or a poorly written sentence in a newspaper or magazine article. These were published in the *New Yorker* as "newsbreaks." For example:

> LOST—Male fox hound, brown head, yellow legs, blue body with large black spots on left side, male. Also female, white with red head and spot on hip.—Fayette (Mo.) *Democrat Leader*.

White's tag line was:

> Those aren't dogs, those are nasturtiums.

After his relationship with Alice broke up, Andy had several girlfriends. In 1926 he thought he was in love again and he wrote a number of poems to the young woman before he ended the friendship. At the magazine he worked closely with Katharine Angell, who was bright and energetic. As hard as she worked, she always found time to encourage him and the other writers she edited. She particularly valued

Finally he took his mother apart, and tried to reason with her.—*Edith Wharton in "The Writing of English."*

Mechanically inclined.

One of White's newsbreaks from the New Yorker

Tag line by E. B. White. Artwork by O. Soglow. © The New Yorker Magazine, Inc. Reprinted by special permission. All rights reserved.

White's writing for the magazine. As their friendship grew stronger, Andy realized Katharine was becoming an important part of his life. He began writing poems to her.

Andy knew she was not happy in her marriage. In June 1928 he sailed for Europe and met Katharine in Paris. They traveled together to Saint Tropez and Corsica, where they had wonderful times, but when they returned to New York they decided not to see each other except at work. Andy continued to write poems about his growing love for Katharine, his sadness and loneliness without her.

By the following May, Katharine had decided to get a divorce from Ernest Angell. She felt that their two children were being harmed by the constant fighting and misunderstandings between them. Insisting that Andy was not the reason for her decision, she took a train to Reno, Nevada, where she had to stay for three months in order to get divorce papers. During the months she was away, the two of them corresponded frequently.

On May 1 Harper and Brothers published a book of sixty-four poems Andy had written from 1923–1929, called *The Lady Is Cold*. His reviews were excellent. At the same time, he was growing dissatisfied with his demanding writing schedule on the *New Yorker*, a weekly magazine. He had to have his editorial columns ready every few days; and besides editorials, he wrote all manner of things for the magazine, from captions for cartoons, to tag lines after newsbreaks, to "Talk of the Town" column pieces. It meant he was always under pressure.

He decided to cut back his responsibilities by spending the summer as a counselor at Camp Otter in Ontario, Canada, because it was a relief to be with young people, enjoying

Andy and campers at Camp Otter, 1921

nature, canoeing, hiking, and singing around the campfire. He had been a counselor at Camp Otter when he was a Cornell student, and he found it a peaceful and satisfying setting, where his hay fever didn't bother him, and he felt as young and carefree as the campers. It was like being a boy at Belgrade Lakes all over again.

When he returned to New York in September, Katharine was back from Reno with her final divorce papers. She and Andy continued to work together on the magazine. They also continued to discuss whether they should get married. Katharine kept reminding him that she had two young children and was seven years older than he was.

Andy no longer feared losing his freedom as he had before.

He also didn't seem to mind the age difference between them or the responsibility of becoming a stepparent to two children. He was in love with Katharine. He was not sure when it had happened, but one day he had gone out of her office and then returned. When he looked at her face, he knew it was true love he was feeling.

A formal portrait of Katharine, 1929 (Nicholas Muray)

—— 8 ——

MARRIAGE

*O*n a Wednesday morning in November 1929, Katharine and Andy were still discussing their future when they abruptly decided to get married that very day. It meant canceling all their other plans, taking a quick trip to city hall for the license, rushing to Katharine's apartment to get Daisy, her Scottish terrier who could not be left alone all day, and driving fifty miles to Bedford Village, one of Katharine's favorite places in the country. There they found a Presbyterian minister who agreed to marry them while Daisy stayed at the house with the minister's dog.

Katharine and Andy were married in a short, no-nonsense ceremony, and after separating the two dogs, who were not getting along, they turned around and drove right back to

New York for dinner. They went back to work at the *New Yorker* offices the next day. A honeymoon would have to wait until the spring, when they could both get away from work.

Andy had always sent Katharine memos in the office and he did not stop once they were married. It was still easier for him to express his deepest feelings on paper; sometimes he even pretended Daisy was doing the writing. Andy also continued to write poems for Katharine. Shortly after they were married, Andy had to be away overnight. Alone in his hotel room, he thought of nothing but Katharine and out of his loneliness he created "Natural History" for her.

Natural History

The spider, dropping down from twig,
Unwinds a thread of his devising:
A thin, premeditated rig
To use in rising.

And all the journey down through space,
In cool descent, and loyal-hearted,
He builds a ladder to the place
From which he started.

Thus I, gone forth, as spiders do,
In spider's web a truth discerning,
Attach one silken strand to you
For my returning.

For each of them, the spider's thread would be an important symbol. Andy would one day write a book about a special spider whose spinning lines are memorable, and often he would refer to the lines Katharine sent out to her friends, many of them *New Yorker* writers she edited.

No matter how much they cared for each other, Andy

knew their marriage was going to be complicated. After all, Katharine's children were not happy to see their parents' marriage end. And he realized it would take time for Nancy and Roger to get used to him and the new marriage. They decided to live in Katharine's apartment at 16 East Eighth Street, where they cut a stairway through the ceiling of the living room into an upstairs apartment to gain extra space.

In the 1920s divorce was not as common as it would become. It was also rare for a mother not to be given complete custody of the children. But Katharine's lawyer may have realized her husband would cause a terrible legal battle if Katharine tried to keep the children. Instead she agreed to joint custody, which meant they would live with her on weekends and holidays and stay with their father during the week. At the time, Nancy was twelve and Roger, nine.

While all these changes were going on in his own life, Andy was troubled by conditions he saw around him. In the United States there was economic depression, with many people out of work. Although he was earning a decent salary, he still remembered what it was like when he could not find a job, how it affected his every thought and made him feel worthless, and how lucky he had been to have a roof over his head and food to eat, even if they belonged to his parents. He was also concerned with the conditions in Europe, where there was growing totalitarianism. He worried about the threat to individual freedom and somehow sensed it would affect the rest of the world.

He and Katharine tried to find ways to deal with the changes in their lives. In the summer Katharine took her children back to Bedford Village, which gave them a country setting not too far from New York City, while Andy went

The farmhouse in North Brooklin, 1990

back to Camp Otter. He sent her letters filled with descriptions of his favorite sights and the daily antics of the young campers. He told Katharine about his exciting discovery of a loon mother with a day-old chick and an unhatched egg. She would be able to share it with him because he set up the tripod and took moving pictures of the excited mother trying to distract him from her nest. He missed Katharine terribly, he said, and sympathized with the lovesick croaking of the noisy frogs every night.

In July Thurber spent two weeks with him at camp and together they put out a newspaper, *Otter Bee*, illustrated with Thurber's zany animals and a man struggling with a canoe that gets the better of him. As comfortable as Andy was in the water and the woods, Thurber was scared of both. But Thurber was able to laugh at his fears in his drawings.

When Andy learned that Katharine was pregnant, he was so excited and emotional he couldn't speak. He had to rely on Daisy to express his feelings of love for her. In a note to a friend, he wrote, "the nursery is in order—ping pong table, commode, drawers with little shirts laid neatly." He was elated at the idea of having a child and felt it would also give him a wonderful alibi in his later years. If he didn't produce enough good writing, he could always say that he had been too busy raising his child.

Joel White was born in December 1930, to the delight of his parents. Again Andy had Daisy write a note for him welcoming his tiny son to the world and telling him to hurry home to see the blooming spring bulbs Katharine had waiting for him. Andy brought the baby home to East Eighth Street and spent all his free time with him in Washington Square Park, because Katharine was hospitalized for an infection and kept in bed for six weeks afterward. He bragged to his friends that he was taking care of all Joel's needs, even mixing a fine formula.

In the summer of 1931 Andy and Katharine rented a cottage in Maine to which they brought all the children. Roger and Nancy were beginning to accept Andy and found it fun to be with their new baby brother. There was an atmosphere of laughter and Andy was patient with them and willing to join in their activities.

In December Andy wrote to his friend that Joel "walks now, a bit of mischief he picked up only last week—from associating with elders. He is a handsome, enthusiastic son and we get on well. We celebrate his first birthday next Monday with cake, prayers, and thanksgiving."

Katharine and Andy had found Maine a soothing place

to be after their hectic New York schedules and they decided to search for a place of their own. In the fall of 1933 they found the perfect spot—a farmhouse in North Brooklin, with twelve rooms, a barn, a boathouse, and nearly forty acres of land surrounding it. The land went right out to the water where "gulls scream their heads off and hair-seals bark like old love-sick terriers," Andy told his brother Stan. It was the perfect place for them. "It looks like the kind of a house a writer would live in," he decided.

In October 1934 Harper's published *Every Day Is Saturday*, Andy's "Notes and Comments" from the *New Yorker*, 1928–1934. The book received excellent reviews, although about the same time a negative article came out saying that White ignored social problems and realities in his editorials in the magazine. Andy was always questioning his value as a writer, and this criticism made him feel he was a terrible failure. He also worried because he had not yet written important works.

He found himself growing tired of writing editorial "Notes and Comments," having to say "we did this" or "we thought that." He wanted to write about issues, saying "I believe this" or "I believe that," and sign his name to it.

In a poem, "I Paint What I See," Andy chose to write about a controversial New York event. Painter Diego Rivera had completed a large mural on the RCA Building in which he had included a portrait of the Russian leader, Lenin. Nelson Rockefeller, who commissioned the mural, insisted Rivera remove Lenin because he represented communism. Rivera offered to add a portrait of Abe Lincoln to balance things. Rockefeller said that would not do. Rivera said he would not remove Lenin.

I Paint What I See

"What do you paint, when you paint on a wall?"
  Said John D.'s grandson Nelson.
"Do you paint just anything there at all?
"Will there be any doves, or a tree in fall?
"Or a hunting scene, like an English hall?"

  "I paint what I see," said Rivera.

"What are the colors you use when you paint?"
  Said John D.'s grandson Nelson.
"Do you use any red in the beard of a saint?
"If you do, is it terribly red, or faint?
"Do you use any blue? Is it Prussian?"

  "I paint what I paint," said Rivera.

"Whose is that head that I see on my wall?"
  Said John D.'s grandson Nelson.
"Is it anyone's head whom we know, at all?
. . . .
"I paint what I think," said Rivera.
. . . .
"However . . .
  "I'll take out a couple of people drinkin'
  "And put in a picture of Abraham Lincoln;
  "I could even give you McCormick's reaper
  "And still not make my art much cheaper,
  "But the head of Lenin has got to stay.
. . . .
"It's not good taste in a man like me,"
  Said John D.'s grandson Nelson.
"To question an artist's integrity
. . . .
"You painted a radical. I say shucks,
  "I never could rent the offices—

"The capitalistic offices.
"For this, as you know, is a public hall
"And people want doves, or a tree in fall,
"And though your art I dislike to hamper,
　"I owe a *little* to God and Gramper,
　"And after all,
　"It's *my* wall . . ."

"We'll see if it is," said Rivera.

The poem is a dialogue between the artist and the businessman, which Andy called "A Ballad of Artistic Integrity." There was no question that Andy believed writers and artists should be free to express their opinions and should not be limited by politics or financial influences. Yet in this instance it turned out that the artist did not have freedom. Rockefeller owned the wall and he had the mural covered over. Rivera could do nothing about it. Andy felt badly, but at least he had been able to speak out through his poem. He added the hope that "in some far away century that mural may turn up again; it will be discovered, probably by a dinosaur looking for a good place to lay some eggs."

As happy as he was in his personal life with Katharine and little Joel, Andy still needed the freedom to pick up and leave. Sometimes he completed a writing project while he was away, sometimes he did not, but Katharine accepted this. She understood that creative people have special needs and she encouraged Andy to do what was required for his writing. Once she wrote him, "It's almost worth having you go away to have your letters which are so wonderful, though I admit I'd rather have *you* than the letters."

For several years he continued to write for the *New Yorker* and to complain about doing so. In 1935 Andy's father died, a close friend died, and Katharine had a miscarriage. The following year his mother died. He was left feeling very sad about the losses in his life and found his own physical problems getting worse. He suffered from stomach problems, dizziness, ear troubles, and, always, hay fever.

He felt he needed to make some changes in his life. After thinking about it for some time, he decided to take a year off. First he wrote a long letter to Katharine, trying to explain what he would *not* do with "My Year," without saying what he would do. He told her he was not using his talents nor was he having fun at his job anymore. It was hard to enjoy writing when you had to meet deadlines, he said. Because he barely finished writing the columns for one issue when it was time to begin the columns for the next issue, he didn't have the time to produce important work. If death could take you at any time, he wanted to try to write something he could be proud of before it did.

He wrote a farewell in the magazine in early August 1937 and then took his boat *Astrid* sailing in Maine. When Katharine and Joel left for New York, Andy stayed on in Maine and began writing a long poem, "Zoo Revisited: Or the Life and Death of Olie Hackstaff." For the poem, he made trips back to Mount Vernon, to Belgrade Lakes, to the zoo, looking at his early settings and trying to use his memories to explain his life, past, present, and future.

Even the choice of his character's name, Hackstaff, referred to the way he saw himself: Merely a hack, or a staff writer who works for a paycheck instead of for literary ends.

In the spring he bought a bird, a female canary who was sitting on an egg. He already had Joel's male bird and Buttercup, another female. In the fall he wrote Katharine about the spectacular color the maple tree had turned and how brilliant the northern lights had appeared in the sky. He wished she were sharing them with him and sent her a crimson maple leaf and the last pansy of the year. He was taking care of everything on the farm and trying to keep a strict writing schedule from nine to one. When he found it was making him irritable, he gave it up, telling Katharine, he "had never written anything between nine and one anyway." By the end of October he returned to New York. It was lonely with only his birds to keep him company.

Confused about what he was doing, he wrote to his friend James Thurber in January 1938, "I have made an unholy mess out of this 'year off' business. I haven't produced two cents worth of work, have broken my wife's health, my own spirit, and two or three fine old lampshades by getting my feet tangled in the cord."

Thurber answered, "You may be a writer in farmer's clothing but you are still a writer...."

The farmhouse was being remodeled in the spring and when Andy saw how many men were working on it, he panicked and rushed back to his typewriter to write "Notes and Comments" for the *New Yorker* again. He was also ready to get back to newsbreaks. Thurber was right. No matter what else he did, farming or sailing, he still had to write. His "year off" had lasted from August 1937 to April 1938.

9

MOVE TO MAINE

*A*ndy and seven-year-old Joel had spent the Christmas of 1937 together in Maine. Like two boys, they had tramped through the snow, gone skating on the pond, visited their new friends, and had found Maine a grand place to be in the winter, as well as the summer. More than ever, White wanted to live there all year round. He loved the people and the place.

By the spring of 1938, he was able to convince Katharine they should move. He gave up his weekly column in the *New Yorker*, with its editorial "we," and signed a contract to write a monthly column for *Harper's Magazine,* using his own name. He did agree to continue editing newsbreaks and to write

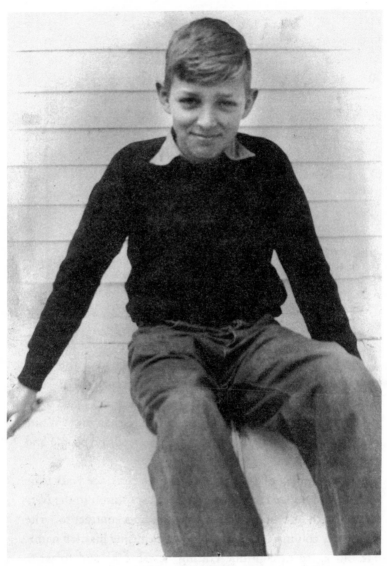

Ten-year-old Joel, 1940

several other pieces for the *New Yorker*, whenever he was inspired.

Because the new column was a monthly, he explained to Ross, he would have a few weeks off between writing each one, time he could use for "shingling a barn or sandpapering an old idea."

Katharine had been working full-time at the *New Yorker* for twelve years. It would be difficult for her to leave the office and to work only part-time, but she said she was willing to make the change for Andy. And she did not see why she could not continue to work for the magazine from Maine. Once the farmhouse was modernized, they would each have a large study in the front of the house.

White knew his hay fever was terrible on the farm, but he was willing to put up with it. "I would really rather feel bad in Maine than good anywhere else," he wrote a friend.

He bought sheep, pullets, geese, roosters, and a pig, and of course, life became much more complicated with this menagerie to care for. He also decided to build a stone wall because that's what literary people were supposed to do. He liked doing farm chores and found them a good excuse when he didn't feel like writing.

The public liked what he wrote in his monthly columns, and subscriptions to *Harper's* increased. Interspersed with the details of his daily chores, or his latest aches and pains, he commented about what was going on in the world. While repairing the roof, he was also worrying about what Hitler was doing all the way across the world. He read and reread Hitler's words and warned that Hitler did not look at an individual as valuable, only as something to be led. As uncertain as he had been about the United States entering the

First World War, he felt strongly that Hitler had to be stopped and the United States had to help stop him. If he had an army, he said, he would have "started fighting Hitler years ago when he was just beginning to be a nuisance."

Andy's readers were interested in his personal problems too. They worried about his aching neck, or why his hens were not producing as many eggs as they usually did. And those readers wrote to tell him how to treat his neck and his chickens.

He and Katharine became very involved in community activities. Often Andy did not have time to sit down and do newsbreaks or work on his columns. Instead he had to drive several hours back and forth to pick up popcorn boxes for the PTA or pack up all the children's books Katharine had reviewed for the *New Yorker* and was donating to the local library. When they lived in New York, they had never been interested in such things, but in a small community, you were expected to participate.

Joel went to school in a two-room schoolhouse, and although he had been worried in the beginning, he quickly made the adjustment from city to country. When Andy asked him what he thought after they had lived in Maine for a time, Joel said he liked it there, the day went quicker in the country—"Just like lightning."

In the evenings the three of them began reading aloud together. It took them about three months to complete *Little Women,* which Andy described as their "after-dinner mint" in the winter months when it was very cozy to sit in front of a fire, listening to another family's trials and tribulations.

The following summer he and Joel took another trip together, this time to Belgrade Lakes. Andy, trying to enjoy every moment of the present, would find himself slipping back to the past. While they were fishing on the lake, he looked at Joel and saw himself as a boy thirty years earlier, in the same rowboat and with the same dragonfly landing on his rod. When he blinked he became his father, sitting at the other end of the rowboat, expectantly waiting for the bass to bite. A few seconds later he was himself again, clutching his fishing rod.

This kept happening, whether they were exploring the shore, drinking their Moxie, or hiking to dinner. Andy kept wondering who he really was. He wrote a moving essay, "Once More to the Lake," in which he described the confusion of moving back and forth between his past and his future, and the fear that he was closer to the end of his life than ever before.

But when he was back on the farm, he found he had energy for everything. For years, he and Katharine had talked about putting together a book of American humor, and they wrote to friends asking for their favorite funny stories. They both read as many as they could and finally selected two hundred pieces beginning with Benjamin Franklin, Mark Twain, Don Marquis, some of White's own work, and many of Thurber's pieces.

The collection turned into an eight-hundred-page anthology for which White wrote an introduction giving his ideas about humor and the writers he and Katharine admired. White felt humor could not be analyzed or dissected. If taken apart and studied, it would never fit together again in the same way. He wanted readers to enjoy the stories and to recognize that humor could be made up of many emotions, including happiness and sadness. When the book was published in November 1941, almost fifteen thousand copies were sold within a few weeks.

Shortly after that, the United States went to war against Germany and Japan, and Andy became a civil defense leader. During practice air raids, he had to don his white helmet and drive along the roads, blowing his horn. As a school patrol-man, Joel had important duties, too, and had to wear a white belt and silver badge, which he rarely took off, even at home. On Christmas Day, 1942, Andy was on duty at his spotting post watching for enemy planes. There were only about four hundred people in the town of North Brooklin at that time, and he felt he was protecting all of them from the enemy.

Earlier that year his *Harper's* columns were brought out as a book called *One Man's Meat,* which received excellent reviews. One critic called him "our finest essayist, perhaps our only one." He continued to write the columns until the following year.

Then in March of 1943 Andy decided he wanted to quit. He was worried about his health and was finding it more difficult to get the essays written each month. *Harper's* editors tried to persuade him to continue, but Andy would not change his mind. He told his friends he'd had a "nervous crack-up" that left him with no energy to do anything. The doctor didn't seem to be able to help, but Andy felt a little better when he stopped writing the columns.

From the time he was a college student, he had worried about his health, often exaggerating any symptoms he might have. Nineteen-year-old Elwyn had written in his journal that if his cough were due to tuberculosis, he would leave Cornell and spend his last months traveling about the country.

Now he was feeling depressed and told his brother Stanley he seemed to have "mice in the subconscious and spurs in the cervical spine." The doctor could find nothing wrong, but that didn't matter to White. He was convinced he was about to die.

Nor did the world situation help him feel better. Ever since the United States had entered the war in 1941, he had worried about young men dying in battles overseas. He had long believed a world government was the only answer, and in the 1943 Christmas issue of the *New Yorker* he published a story about the aftermath of a terrible war. In it, there were only a few people left in the world, and when they came together, a delegate from China brought a kind of iris, called a wild flag, and suggested that all countries adopt the flower as the symbol of world unity. It was more than a story to White. It became a passionate dream.

Many of the people on the *New Yorker* staff had joined the armed forces and Katharine and Andy decided they were needed back in New York to help out on the magazine. They left Maine and moved into a furnished apartment, sending Joel off to boarding school in February 1944.

By then, both Nancy and Roger had graduated from college. As an undergraduate, Nancy attended Bryn Mawr, Katharine's alma mater, and she later received her Ph.D. in biology, which was startling to her mother. Roger graduated from Harvard and joined the air force. Katharine and Andy encouraged his love for writing and were pleased when he chose to become a writer and *New Yorker* editor. That seemed more understandable to Katharine than Nancy's choice of a scientific field.

Later that year Katharine and Andy found an apartment in the Village on West Eleventh Street, only a block from where Andy had lived with his Cornell fraternity brothers years before. It felt wonderful to be back in a setting with such fond memories.

——10——

STUART LITTLE

*I*n the spring of 1939 Andy had sent his editor some pages he had been working on for a children's story about Stuart Little, a tiny creature wearing a hat and twirling a cane, who had come to him in a dream twelve years earlier. Over the years he had been telling Stuart stories to all his nieces and nephews, and once Joel was old enough, he began telling them to Joel. He was not good at making them up on the spot. Instead he wrote down his ideas whenever they occurred to him.

Only recently had he thought they might become a book. But he was not rushing it. "I would rather wait a year than publish a bad children's book," he told his editor, "as I have too much respect for children." When the time came, he hoped they would find an illustrator who understood Stuart and could portray him well.

The book idea was put away while Andy worked on the farm and wrote his pieces for the *New Yorker* and *Harper's*. Now that he and Katharine were back in New York in the winter of 1944, he found the city invigorating. He remembered how he had spent those earlier years exploring its every corner, from the waterfront to Central Park, from the Hudson River to the Lower East Side. It seemed the perfect time for him to pull out the children's story. He discovered that it needed very little work and within two months he had completed the final version. It came together very quickly without any research or special study.

When *Stuart Little* was published in October 1945, Andy saw people of all ages reading it on the bus, or buying it in bookstores. Everywhere he looked, there was Stuart, rowing his canoe through the cornfields, as he had been depicted by the illustrator, Garth Williams. Williams had captured Stuart perfectly, from the hats he wore on his head down to the shoes he wore on his feet. Andy was pleased the book was selling well, because he wanted to provide Katharine with funds if something happened to him. He always expected something terrible to happen to him.

Over the years the popularity of the book has not waned. By the late 1970s more than two and a half million copies were sold and it had been translated into twenty languages. In the 1990s teachers are still using the book in classrooms to describe true friendship and artful writing.

But just before the book came out, there was some controversy over it. A New York librarian was distressed by the story of a mouse being born into a human family and she told Andy not to publish the book. He was adamant that children would like the story, saying "children can sail easily over the fence that separates reality from make-believe." Katharine wrote to the librarian that she thought it was a very funny book and that children would love it and so would their parents. She felt the story had enough humor, satire, philosophy, and beauty that it would be enjoyed on many levels by all ages.

Stuart is as tiny as a mouse and certainly resembles a mouse with his long, skinny tail, but White kept insisting that his publishers not use the term in their publicity about the book. He did not think of Stuart as a mouse; he called Stuart a "second son." Because of his size, Stuart is able to help his family by squeezing into small spots, retrieving Ping-Pong balls, and unsticking piano keys. Yet when Stuart's adventures begin, his family quickly fades into the background, and he's on his own, as many young readers wish they could be.

Stuart has special miniature clothes, furniture, and money, and must always be on the lookout for danger from cats and dogs. But his world is not limited by his size. He has E. B. White's philosophy and sense of humor. Just like White, he loves to be the first person up to enjoy the early morning quiet and the "fresh smell of day." Also, like the sailor White was, Stuart loves to be on the waves with the "breeze in his face and the cry of the gulls overhead. . . ."

When Stuart substitutes for a teacher who is out ill with "rhinestones," he asks the students what is important to them. Again we hear echoes of White: "A shaft of sunlight at the

TOM TRIKKELBOUT

door

E. B. WHITE *en*
GODFRIED BOMANS

DE BEZIGE BIJ · AMSTERDAM

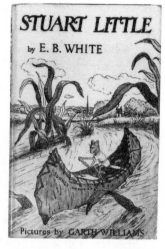

STUART LITTLE

by E. B. WHITE

Pictures by GARTH WILLIAMS

E. B. WHITE
LE AVVENTURE
DI STUART LITTLE

MIGLIARESI · ROMA

E. B. WHITE

Knatten

RABEN & SJÖGREN

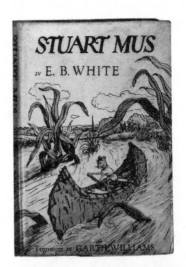

Stuart Little *book jackets with different illustrations and different languages*

end of a dark afternoon, a note in music, and the way the back of a baby's neck smells if its mother keeps it tidy," and, of course, ice cream. These are the important things in life, they all agree. They even talk a bit about world government, one of White's favorite ideas.

Stuart's date with Harriet is a total disappointment. The canoe he lovingly prepares for their ride has been destroyed, and he is not willing to do anything else during their time together. He sits and sulks, refusing to accept one of Harriet's peppermints, refusing to have dinner with her, or to go dancing at the country club.

White had early disappointments on dates, also: the time he took Eileen tea dancing in New York, when he could not veer from his exact plans for that day, or his experience with Alice, when he wasn't ready for a permanent relationship. Like White, Stuart is determined to continue his search for an elusive Margalo, not to get sidetracked in Ames' Crossing with a real-life girl who is just his size.

Stuart became a real person to children, not a creature from the pages of a book. One young reader sent Andy a tiny pair of skates for Stuart. Others followed Stuart's search for Margalo, the lovely brown bird "with a streak of yellow on her bosom," hoping he would find her. But many readers, young and old, had trouble with this ending, and wrote to White, asking him whether Stuart ever found his friend and his fortune. White always replied that it didn't matter. His book was the story of a quest and any direction Stuart chose had to be the right one, no matter what he found.

White, like Stuart, was searching for something in his own life. By writing a children's book that was popular for young and old, he saw that he had finally created an "Original Work." It was written during a time when White felt depressed and worried about his health, and yet many find it one of his funniest books. The success of *Stuart Little* should have lifted his depression, but it did not.

——11——

NEW YORK AGAIN

*A*ndy worried about his own health, Katharine's health, and the health of the world. Once World War II was over, he added a new worry—nuclear destruction. He was filled with visions of the destruction atomic bombs had caused when dropped on Japan. He saw firsthand the chaos at the United Nations, whose headquarters were close to their New York apartment. He could not turn off any of these worries, and decided to speak with a psychiatrist again, as he had done a few years earlier.

We know that he often wrote about himself, and in his story "The Second Tree from the Corner," we see Mr. Trexler (or Andy) after a visit to his psychiatrist, questioning the doctor's need for a larger home and more material items.

Andy realizes those are not what he is seeking. He does not need a larger house, or a fancier boat, or a faster car. His desire is as basic as the second tree from the corner and as difficult to achieve. In writing *Stuart Little,* he had found it for a moment, but as a writer, his search could not end with one creation. He would have to continue the quest.

Andy may not have felt physically content, but his work was winning awards as well as increasing his audience. In 1945 he won a gold medal for *One Man's Meat,* the book of his *Harper's* essays, and the following year the Newspaper Guild gave him the Page One Award for his *New Yorker* editorials. He did not attend ceremonies for any of these awards and even refused membership in the National Institute of Arts and Letters, saying he was a nonjoiner.

The summer of 1946 was a tonic for Andy when the family came together again in Maine. Joel was home from school and because Maine allowed fifteen-year-olds to have their driver's licenses, he wanted to learn to drive. Andy found an old Model T for him to learn on. With its rumble seat converted to wooden panels, and a new canvas top, the vintage car must have been the envy of his friends. Once he had mastered driving it, Joel also wanted to take the family's convertible out, and that meant his parents did not sleep at night until he was safely home. Andy described how he sat waiting, his bones growing more brittle by the minute, while Joel, with his soft bones, was out enjoying himself.

Earlier he had taught his stepdaughter Nancy how to drive, and before that, he had taken Katharine out for lessons. No matter how often the gears were stripped, the brakes were jolted, or the motor killed, Andy kept his good humor.

How quickly the years were passing. It seemed just yesterday that Joel had started walking, and now he was driving. Just a moment before, when he was eleven, the two of them had been building Joel's first boat together. Their design for the small scow came from Andy's *American Boys Handy Book*, complete with drawings and a list of materials they would need.

They started with native cedar, planing it smooth, while the fragrant shavings curled around their feet. They carefully sanded the wood, joined it with sunken nails and caulking, and then painted it. Katharine christened it *Flounder* with a bottle of ginger ale as Joel pushed off to sea on the frog pond below their farmhouse. Joel got his sea legs in that small scow on their pond. When Andy thought he was ready, Joel graduated to wider waters. He grew up to graduate from MIT as a naval architect, to design and build handsome wooden boats in a boatyard only a few minutes away from the saltwater farm.

In Maine, summers came to an end with the Blue Hill Fair. That year Andy and Katharine tramped through the fairground, looking at the livestock and food exhibits; Joel and a date saw the fair from the top of the Ferris wheel. In a few years, Andy would use the fairground as a model for the one in *Charlotte's Web*, where Wilbur wins his medal and Fern takes a romantic ride with Henry Fussy.

In the fall, Joel went back to school and Katharine and Andy went back to New York and the magazine. Andy's book *The Wild Flag* came out that winter, and he wrote to his brother Stan, "In it I make my debut as a THINKER. . . ." The book was made up of his *New Yorker* comments about world government and the articles he had written when the magazine sent him to San Francisco to cover the drafting of the United Nations Charter in May 1945. In it he included

Andy and Katharine at work, 1940s

his idea that the wild iris might become a symbol for the whole world, rather than each country waving its own flag and calling for its own solutions. He was convinced that world government was the best answer for the future of the human race.

In the summer, Andy had written to Stan that the doctor told him he would feel better if he quit writing. For Christmas, Stan sent him a box of white bond paper as though to remind him how important his writing was. The gift did just that. Thanking Stan, Andy described how "a blank sheet of paper holds the greatest excitement there is for me. . . . I can remember . . . looking a sheet of paper square in the eyes when

I was seven or eight years old and thinking 'This is where I belong, this is it.' " Again, he did not sound like a man who had decided to give up writing, even if his doctor recommended he do so. Writing was something he had to do, like eating or breathing.

Andy often wrote a story when he was troubled by an event in his life. Sometimes it helped him to solve a problem or make sense of an idea. While they were still in Maine, Andy had been raising a pig he intended to kill for its bacon and pork roasts when it was full grown. That's how one lived on a farm, by raising animals and crops for food. Eggs were eaten or sold. Chickens were cooked for dinner. Corn was picked for meals. Fruit was preserved.

But when his pig got sick, Andy spent many hours with it, trying desperately to keep it alive. It didn't make sense to him at all. He began to wonder about the way things happen. He also began to ask questions about his own life and death. In the story "Death of a Pig," he expressed his troubled reactions, but he did not get over the pig's death.

Andy rarely raised his voice or lost his temper with his family and friends. But when he saw injustice in the world, he could not remain calm. In November 1947 he wrote a strong letter to the *New York Herald Tribune* criticizing its editorial which approved the firing of Hollywood people who refused to answer questions before the House Committee on Un-American Activities. "I can only assume that your editorial writer, in a hurry to get home for Thanksgiving, tripped over the First Amendment and thought it was the office cat," he wrote.

He felt strongly that the Constitution gives individuals the right to believe what they want and to belong to any organization or church of their choice. No one should have to sign a loyalty oath in order to keep a job. "If I must declare today that I am not a Communist," he insisted, "tomorrow I shall have to testify that I am not a Unitarian. And the day after, that I never belonged to a dahlia club." He ended by saying, "It is not a crime to believe anything at all in America."

The newspaper responded with another strong editorial saying Andy was a "dangerous . . . element" in society. Again he countered that no matter what else was happening, the United States had to "continue to apply our civil rights and duties equally to all citizens, even to citizens of opposite belief. This may be a dangerous and false idea, but my holding it does not necessarily make me a dangerous and false man. . . ." Supreme Court Justice Felix Frankfurter wrote Andy to congratulate him for standing up to the newspaper with such strong words.

By January 1948, when he wrote Stan about all the controversy with the newspaper and people's strong reaction to the pig story, he admitted that his head was feeling better. But now Katharine was having trouble with her spine and would not stop working long hours on the magazine.

Katharine and Andy had numerous physical ailments. They talked about them a great deal and wrote about them to their family and friends. Some people called them hypochondriacs. Even good friends made fun. Thurber wrote that Andy "expects every day of his life that something will kill him: a bit of mold, a small bug, a piece of huckleberry pie." But many of their ailments were real and often difficult to live with. They just had to learn to ignore the teasing.

In April, Katharine had back surgery. The surgeon spliced a bone from her pelvis into her spine, and she spent many weeks wearing a brace. By the following summer, she was fit enough to get back to her gardening.

White received an honorary degree from Dartmouth that year and surprisingly chose to attend the ceremony, taking Joel with him when Katharine was unable to travel. But it did not go well. He wrote Katharine from the campus that night telling her that it had been a very difficult evening for him. He was uncomfortable with strangers and still fearful of platforms. It was the same old fear he carried with him from grammar school.

Now he had the added concern that when he ate, he "filled up immediately with gas and apprehension," and when he didn't eat, he suffered from "emptiness and dizziness and vapors." No wonder he preferred to stay at home.

This time, he wrote Katharine, when the big moment came at the ceremony for them to slip the honorary hood over his head, it slipped and covered his whole face. No one had told him to attach the hood to his jacket and he felt ridiculous. But somehow, Andy managed to accept two additional honorary degrees that same summer, from Yale and the University of Maine, and he finally mastered the wearing of hoods.

Before he left New York, he bought a new pair of shoes for wearing on special occasions and decided to break them in by going to one of his favorite places, the Bronx Zoo. He walked along watching the animals, until suddenly he stopped. Right in front of him a red doe had just given birth to a fawn. The newborn rose on shaky legs, and then he saw a second fawn curled up and wet from birth. He described with awe how the sun seemed to be highlighting the scene, bringing out the twins' white spots against their bright red coats. He moved close to the fence and caressed one of the fawns to make sure it was real.

Other visitors to the zoo walked right past the doe and her fawns. One child noticed them and yelled to his mother to look at the "kangaroos," but no one else was looking carefully enough to witness what Andy had seen.

Andy was asked to write an article for *Holiday* magazine about New York City, which he did, and which later was issued as a small book. In it he describes his fond memories of the city and his worries as he watches it changing and growing less friendly.

Andy and Katharine's life in New York was pleasant, although never as satisfying for Andy as the farm in Maine. He did find their latest apartment with its Turtle Bay Gardens very lovely in spring when tulips, hyacinths, daffodils, and apple blossoms flooded the setting, and the white-throated sparrows and hermit thrushes came to enjoy them.

In 1951 the *Holiday* magazine editor asked Andy to travel cross-country, as he had done after college, and write about his experiences. He agreed to go and started out with enthusiasm, but by the time he reached Pennsylvania he was ready to turn back. The traffic was heavy, it moved with great speed, and he realized he could not repeat that earlier experience. There were now major highways crossing the country from east to west and from north to south, and everyone was on them. When he had taken his earlier trip west, there were few automobiles on the road and a person could travel at a leisurely pace. Change was taking place everywhere, not just in New York City.

That December, Harold Ross died. Andy and Katharine both felt very dejected about losing such a close friend and valuable *New Yorker* colleague. They realized the magazine would never be quite the same without the man who had created it. White wrote a moving eulogy, which he called a love letter for his friend, describing how Ross had been able to achieve his dream: "He wanted the magazine to be good, to be funny, and to be fair."

——12——

CHARLOTTE'S WEB

*F*or some time Andy had been thinking about writing another children's story. He knew he wanted to write about the animals in his barn and he definitely wanted to save a pig's life. He had not forgotten how upset he felt when his pig died, how the experience had frightened him. He had found it puzzling that he should fight for the life of a creature that he was raising to kill and eventually eat. It was this puzzle he wanted to explore.

One day Andy was passing through the shed and happened to look up. There was a large gray spider spinning an egg sac. He stopped to watch her as she wound her delicate white line round and round, up and around the eggs she had laid. Leaving for New York a few days later, Andy decided

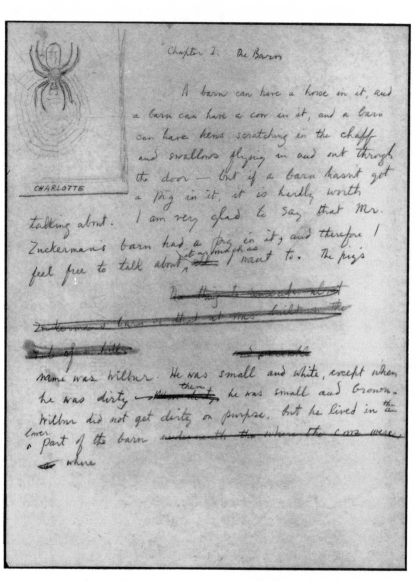

A page from an early version of Charlotte's Web

to take the egg sac with him. He found a box, made air holes in the top, and gently placed the sac inside. After a few weeks, he noticed tiny spiders coming out of the holes in the box and spinning delicate lines all over the objects on his dresser. Andy was thrilled.

He did not know very much about spiders, but now he wanted to learn all about them. In the library he found books that described everything about spiders' habits: what they ate, where they lived, how many kinds there were. Andy was going to call his spider Charlotte, and he wanted to be completely accurate as he described her behavior.

By January 1951 White wrote his editor, Ursula Nordstrom, that he had a story, but he wanted to put it away for a while "to ripen." When he did take it out of the drawer, he wrote and rewrote the beginning, trying to get it just right. This time it did not come together as quickly as *Stuart Little* had. In one early version, he began the story: "Charlotte was a big gray spider who lived in a doorway. But there is no use talking about Charlotte until we have talked about her close friend—a pig named Wilbur."

In another version, he wrote: "A barn can have a horse in it, and a barn can have a cow in it, and a barn can have hens scratching in the chaff and swallows flying in and out through the door—but if a barn hasn't got a pig in it, it is hardly worth talking about."

He continued to write new versions about the barn, and then the spider, and then the pig, and then back to the barn. Piles of yellow paper grew with version after version, until there were nine in all. Finally Andy had a brand-new idea. He added Fern and began the story with Fern asking her mother, "Where's Papa going with that ax?" That was it.

Now he had the beginning, and the rest of the book was ready to come together. He may have had to revise a great deal, but once it was right, he knew it because he heard bells and saw lights.

Andy had never worried about the ending of the story. Those words had been with him from the start: "It is not often that someone comes along who is a true friend and a good writer. Charlotte was both."

By March 1952 he signed a contract for *Charlotte's Web* and by May he was back in Maine with terrible hay fever but still happy to be there. The book came out in the fall and was reviewed everywhere. One reviewer said, "It is just about perfect" and another thought it "the most beautiful and strengthening book" she had read. By 1984 well over 6 million copies were sold, and in 1990 it was selected by three hundred thousand children all around the country as their favorite book, just as it had been in a poll twenty years before.

Charlotte did not come to White in a dream, all in one piece, as Stuart had. Living in Maine for nearly five years gave him daily information about life on a farm and in a barn, and he was shaping ideas in his mind without even knowing it.

In Andy's barn, each of the creatures behaves exactly the way it should in nature. Charlotte sucks the blood of insects and must die after she lays her egg sac. She tells us in a matter-of-fact way about her diet of flies and bugs and says that's just the way her life is. Templeton, the rat, is a selfish scavenger, just the way a rat really is. Wilbur eats his slops and rests in the cool mud, or the fragrant manure, just as pigs do.

The stuttering goose is exactly like the rest of Andy's

gaggle of geese who boss everyone around and hiss their comments about everything that happens on the farm. Even Fern and Avery act like brothers and sisters. Avery teases and shows off. Fern tries to ignore him. Fern begins to grow up and her interest turns from the barn to Henry Fussy after he takes her on the Ferris wheel.

The characters in the story have no problem accepting the magic in their world. Mr. Zuckerman is sure a miracle has occurred and the minister explains that we should always be looking for wonders in our lives. Dr. Dorian thinks spiderwebs are miracles, even without words in them. Most readers have no problem accepting Charlotte, with her kind heart, cultured manner, and sophisticated vocabulary. Of course she is able to spin wonderful adjectives about Wilbur into her web. We don't question that.

And Andy never worried about using long words. "Children are game for anything," he said. "I throw them hard words and they backhand them over the net. They love words that give them a hard time" as long as they are interested in the story.

Wilbur is a very lucky pig. Fern saves his life at birth; Charlotte saves it later by making him famous so that Mr. Zuckerman won't want to slaughter his amazing pig. This time Andy has found a way to save his pig.

Just when readers are ready to feel very sad about Charlotte's dying alone on the deserted fairground, they understand she is a heroine who will never be forgotten. Her relatives will continue to be born on the farm, and there will be a few spiders from each generation who stay to keep Wilbur company.

Twenty years after *Charlotte's Web* was published, parents

wrote to tell Andy how much they had loved the book when they were children. Now they were reading it to their children. Instead of feeling pleased, Andy felt old when he got such letters, except when his great-grandson Sam, at age four, wrote his own version of the book and added "crunchy" to the list of adjectives. Wilbur might not have liked his choice of words, but Andy certainly did.

—13—

THOREAU'S INFLUENCE

*A*ndy's favorite book was Henry David Thoreau's *Walden*. He took it with him everywhere and was constantly turning to one section or another to find an answer to his concerns. He had it on his trip West, and when he lived in Seattle. It joined him on his Alaskan voyage and when he traveled by train to San Francisco for the creation of the United Nations Charter. He wrote, "I keep it about me in much the same way one carries a handkerchief—for relief in moments of defluxion or despair."

Andy gave *Walden* to the important people in his life: to his friends, to Katharine, to their grandchildren for Christmas. He felt all graduating college students should be given a copy to help them appreciate the simplicity with which Thoreau lived and wrote.

Andy first read *Walden* when he was in college and felt it gave him courage to keep going whenever he questioned his own ability, because Thoreau reminded him, "if one advances confidently in the direction of his dreams . . . he will meet with a success. . . ."

It was the spring of 1845 when Thoreau took an ax and headed for the woods to find a place to build his house. He intended to live alone in nature as simply as possible, while keeping a record of his thoughts and his daily activities, which eventually would become the book *Walden*. Andy said that everyone tried to call Thoreau a naturalist or a hermit or a renegade, but he thought of him as a writer, plain and simple. Not just any kind of writer. "He was the subtlest humorist of the nineteenth century," according to White.

Thoreau loved the land, saying heaven is under our feet as well as over our heads. Both men appreciated the natural world in similar ways. Thoreau wanted a simple life without too many objects or too many people. So did Andy. He valued a few objects, especially his car and his boat, and he liked having his family and friends around him. But Andy shared with Thoreau the need for a great deal of solitude.

In the summer of 1954 White was asked by Yale University to write an essay about Thoreau for the one hundredth anniversary of *Walden*. He wrote the essay in his ten-by-fifteen-foot Maine boathouse, a space similar to the small house Thoreau had built on Walden Pond. White said that he could be himself in the boathouse, his wild and healthy self, and that he created better there than in any other place.

In writing this tribute to Thoreau, White said he was

glad to be able to show his appreciation to the man who had always been there for him when he needed it. He was eager to pass on Thoreau's ideas to those he knew and to anyone else who would listen.

Using Thoreau's philosophy and his own, Andy answered a young woman who wrote him she was unsure of her future. He told her he thought it was very difficult to be young and not know what you are going to do with your life. But eventually "we discard what we don't like, walk away from what fails to inspirit us. My first job was with the United Press, but I knew within half an hour that my heart was not in it and that I would never be any good at gathering straight news under great difficulties and with the clock always running out."

He went on, "we should all do what, in the long run, gives us joy, even if it is only picking grapes or sorting the laundry." He quoted Thoreau: "To affect the quality of the day, that is the highest of arts."

In June 1955 Andy and Katharine traveled by boat to England. They had talked about the trip and planned it for years, but something always interfered. At last they were going. The leisurely crossing was pleasant, but they both found it difficult to manage once they arrived. They were used to their own surroundings in the United States and found their hotel rather stuffy. Andy did not feel comfortable driving on the left side of the road and did not like having to hire a driver at exorbitant rates.

After three weeks in England they decided to sail home, without completing their trip to Germany to visit Joel and his family. Joel had married Allene while he was still in college. After graduation he joined the army and was sent overseas. Katharine and Andy would have liked to visit Joel, Allene, and their three children, but there was a possibility that the stewards on their shipping line would go on strike and they decided not to chance getting stranded. If they found it complicated to travel in a country where they spoke the language, they knew it would be even more difficult in Germany. This turned out to be their last trip abroad.

In the fall Andy stopped writing his weekly column for the *New Yorker* and began writing what he called "letters" from wherever he was. The first one appeared in December 1955 and told about his trip to Maine for the holidays. Another letter was written after he had visited a circus in Florida and watched a young woman rehearsing her act on the back of a horse. For him time stopped, as she performed without makeup, in bare feet, in a ring without music or spotlight. He was seeing the authentic performance that an audience would never know.

Another letter was written after he attended sessions at the United Nations building right near their apartment. Writing the letters was a new challenge, and again he felt he needed the change from weekly deadlines, even though he did not need to travel far to find material for his writing.

When the letters were later combined into a book, *The Points of My Compass,* he wrote on the flap, "I sound off at intervals like a factory whistle.... The trouble with me is, I go around with a chipmunk on my shoulder. This makes me fidget. And my way of fidgeting is to write."

In January 1956 he was having stomach trouble and had to undergo a battery of X rays. The doctor explained that his pylorus, or stomach opening, closed up tight "at the slightest hint of trouble ahead." At last he had a good explanation for not being able to speak in front of groups. He could blame it on what happened to his insides.

Katharine had decided to retire from the *New Yorker,* but the fiction editor died in February, and Katharine was asked to head the fiction department. She agreed to it for a time.

On Andy's fifty-seventh birthday, in July, Katharine and Andy made an early morning trip out to Brooklyn to meet the ship that was bringing Joel, Allene, and the children back to the United States. They stood on the dock, waving and waving, and waiting for what seemed like an hour until the soldiers and their families began disembarking. At last they saw Joel's smiling face. Having his family home was the best birthday present Andy could receive.

——14——

MAINE, YEAR-ROUND

As soon as Joel and his family were settled in Maine, Andy visited them frequently. Each time he went, he was more convinced he and Katharine should leave New York for good. He felt he had lived in eight caves in the city during the past thirty years and that was enough. He knew he would miss certain things about New York, especially their Forty-eighth Street apartment with its lovely courtyard and the thrushes who visited their sweet gum tree in the spring. But now he needed to live in Maine with his family and his farm.

Once again Katharine said she was willing to move back to Maine, as long as she could continue to work for the *New Yorker* part-time. She was getting used to this routine of moving from New York to Maine and back again. She looked forward to working in her garden and would eventually write delightful articles about gardening, and about famous gardens past and present. She also would review new and old gardening books, as well as garden catalogs for the magazine.

Andy continued to write poetry about nature and about Katharine. For one of her birthdays he wrote:

To My American Gardener With Love

Before the seed there comes the thought of bloom,
  The seedbed is the restless mind itself.
Not sun, not soil alone can bring
This rush of beauty and this sense of order.
Flowers respond to something in the gardener's face—
Some secret in the heart, some special grace.
Yours were the rains that made the roses grow,
And that is why I love your garden so.

By December 1957 they were settled in the Maine farmhouse and able to celebrate Christmas surrounded by their children and grandchildren. The farm became a gathering place for the whole family. Roger and Nancy visited whenever they could and brought their families. When they couldn't get to Maine they wrote or called to keep in touch. Joel's family had a home nearby so they could drop in frequently.

Andy wasted no time in again purchasing livestock for the farm. He bought two heifers, sheep, chickens, and geese. He also had a new boat, *Fern*, a twenty-foot double-ender sloop from Denmark on which he planned to sail every free moment. Sometimes he wrote in his study or in the living room, where there was always the activity of household help, a ringing phone, Katharine asking him questions or sending

Andy playing baseball with granddaughter, Martha, 1960

memos as she always had done in the office. "The members of my household never pay the slightest attention to my being a writing man," he told an interviewer. When he needed to be quiet he went out to the boathouse, where he wrote to the sounds of gently lapping waves and the company of a mouse and a nearby woodchuck.

Andy went through the same ordeal each time he wrote the weekly "Notes and Comments" paragraphs for the beginning pages of the *New Yorker*. One whole day was spent getting down his ideas. Then he began revising. He moved a sentence from the middle to the beginning. He took out words. He tightened the sentences. Each version sounded a little better to him. Finally he thought he had it. Slipping the typed yellow page into an envelope addressed to the magazine in New York, he took it to the post office. On the way home, he thought of a better way to express the ending. Turning the car around, he headed back to the post office and tried to persuade the clerk to return his envelope. Sometimes this happened more than once.

It was never easy for him to write these paragraphs or, in fact, any of his other pieces. It always required a struggle. But he wrote the "Notes and Comments" paragraphs, off and on, for thirty years. Sometimes he wrote with pleasure about his trip to the zoo, sometimes he wrote with concern about the world at war or the smoke in our air. No matter what his subject, his words were clear, his ideas strong enough to jar his readers and force them to think. He made them smile. He made them laugh. He made them weep.

Andy wrote an essay on William Strunk, Jr., his professor at Cornell, after a friend sent him a copy of Strunk's *Elements of Style*, which had been known on campus as "the little book." An editor read his article on Strunk in the *New Yorker* and called to ask him to revise the little book and suggested that his essay be used for the introduction. Andy was delighted. He had enjoyed Professor Strunk's English 8 class in 1919 and thought the little book had been useful. He expected it to be easy to revise, telling the editor he would complete the work in just a few months. Once he started, it turned out to be much more complicated than he had realized. He found that he didn't always know the correct rules of grammar, that he had been writing by ear all those years. It meant he would have to go back and learn the rules before he could teach them to anyone else.

After many months of working with Strunk's ideas, Andy

finally finished. He had added an introduction, reorganized the sections of the book, and changed some of the examples of right and wrong usage, but he felt he had retained Strunk's humor and his strong commands. When Andy completed the manuscript in November 1958, the publishers sent it to college professors around the country to get their reactions. Most of them thought the book old-fashioned and wanted Andy to modernize it. He refused. He felt the language had not changed just because so many years had passed. It was still correct to add an apostrophe and an *s* when you were talking about Charles's tonsils, no matter what anyone said. It was not correct to use *like* for *as*: "We spent the evening as in the old days," not "We spent the evening like in the old days."

Apparently Andy's instincts about the book were correct, because it sold well from the beginning and still continues to be a valuable tool for students and writers. Now known affectionately as Strunk and White, it has sold more than five and a half million copies.

On the farm, writing was a small part of Andy's day. He rose early to start a fire in the stove. He fed the hens and geese. He collected and cleaned the eggs, fed the sheep and dogs, filled the woodbox, emptied the garbage, loaded the bird feeder, and laid a fire in the living room. In the evenings, after dinner, he worked on newsbreaks for the *New Yorker*.

Each spring, from his bedroom window, Andy watched a mother raccoon climb up and down the leafy cottonwood in front of their Maine farmhouse. She timed her descent just as the sun was beginning to set. By the time her paw touched the ground, the sun had slipped behind the horizon and she was almost invisible. "A man is lucky, indeed," said Andy,

*Andy preparing mash for the chickens with two-year-old grandson
John Henry Angell, 1972*

if he "lives where sunset and coonset are visible from the same window."

He thought of the raccoon as a member of the family and made sure he woke at three in the morning to watch her climb back up the tree to her kittens. He found he had to compete with her for corn. She not only ate many ears of corn, but ruined many more, looking for the sweetest ones. He realized that he would have to plant more corn, some for her and some for himself.

Often his grandchildren came to visit and help Andy with his chores. He also had help from Henry Allen, who had taken care of things around the place for many years. Sometimes strangers dropped in to see the barn and the creator of *Charlotte's Web*. "They drive right into my driveway," White wrote, "stop the car, get out and start talking about contemporary problems even though I've never laid eyes on them before." White was usually hospitable to those people.

He was not so nice when he saw environmental problems or disagreed with political issues. From his earliest time on the magazine he had been fighting against pollution. In 1927 he wrote an editorial about excessive coal smoke being allowed into the atmosphere. "I believe that *no* chemical waste is the correct amount to discharge into the fresh rivers of the world," he said forcefully, and fumes from factory chimneys should not be allowed into the atmosphere. In the late 1950s and the 1960s he worried there was too much strontium 90 in milk supplies, about insecticides killing birds and turning up in food, about automobile exhausts, about cigarette smoke, and weapons-testing in the atmosphere.

He was never afraid to speak out on what he believed

was right. In 1940 he wrote with concern about Anne Morrow Lindbergh's book supporting Nazi Germany. Later he wrote about Senator Joseph McCarthy's misuse of power when he tried to accuse so many citizens of being Communists. He admired Rachel Carson and felt her book *Silent Spring* was of utmost importance. "It may well be the book by which the human race will stand or fall," he wrote.

He cautioned a big corporation when it paid an author to write a magazine article, saying that companies should not be able to influence a writer's ideas. No one should come between the writer and the magazine. The company told him they had reconsidered and would not do that again. Andy seemed to be able to read the future of politics and environmental issues and often urged caution about the dangers ahead. But he always combined the serious with touches of wit and humor, using his excellent ear for conversation and strong, colorful words.

By January 1961 Katharine decided she was ready to retire from her editorial work on the *New Yorker,* although she intended to continue writing her gardening articles. Until surgery on a blocked neck artery slowed her down, she still managed to keep up her correspondence, sometimes writing a dozen or more letters each day.

Winters in Maine could be extremely cold and snowy. It had become a habit for Katharine and Andy to spend a month in Florida to get away from the chilling weather. That year the doctor advised them to stay away longer because he thought it would be good for Katharine to have the warmth of a southern climate. Andy found it boring living in Florida without all his farm chores, but he put up with it for

Katharine's sake and asked friends to join him for fishing and boating. When Katharine was up to it, they went to baseball games, one of the few activities she really enjoyed.

One evening they attended a lecture given by a friend, but because there was a flu epidemic in the community, both of them wore surgical masks and sat as far away from the rest of the audience as they could. No use taking chances on catching germs if they could avoid it, and there were germs in Florida, even without freezing weather. It became their new routine to spend the winter months in Florida and the rest of the year in Maine.

One July morning in 1963 Andy was in the bathtub when Katharine answered the telephone. The operator had a telegram for E. B. White. Katharine started taking down the lengthy message, word for word. After some time she became suspicious, thinking the whole thing was a joke. Of course it's not a joke, the offended Western Union operator told her. They were not allowed to play practical jokes.

The telegram turned out to be quite authentic. It was sent by President Kennedy to say that Andy had been awarded the Presidential Medal of Freedom for his contribution to the quality of American life. The president was inviting Andy and Katharine to the White House in December, when he would present the medal in a special celebration. Andy was delighted to hear he had been selected for the honor, but he probably began making up excuses for why he would not be able to attend the ceremony as he was getting out of the bathtub, even though the event was five months away.

When President Kennedy was assassinated in November,

Andy wrote a strong piece about the energetic young president for the magazine and sent his sympathy to the president's brother Robert. And he also sent his regrets. He could not possibly go to Washington because Katharine was not well and because the tragedy had left him too saddened.

But this time he could not avoid receiving the award. Senator Edmund Muskie of Maine would not let him. Andy finally agreed to meet the senator at Colby College in Waterville because the president of the college was his friend. He asked Allene to drive with him, took a picnic lunch and a thermos of martinis, and they were off. In the president's living room, the senator placed the ribboned medal over Andy's head, with little fanfare, and Andy returned to Katharine with positive reports about the day and especially about the lovely roses growing outside his friend's home.

The following spring Katharine was still not well. She had to be hospitalized in New York for treatment of a rare and painful skin disease. The medicine she took for her skin later weakened her bones, and sometimes it seemed as though she were facing major problems with her health all the time. Andy worried about her until she felt better and then he began to have his own problem, this time with dizziness.

But this did not keep him from having Joel build him a twenty-foot boat, which he named *Martha,* after his granddaughter. He still loved sailing as much as he always had, even though he was often dizzy, or had arthritic fingers, or ringing in his ears. He could have all those problems on land as well as on the sea, and he preferred to be out on the water.

As the years passed, Katharine continued to write her ten to twelve letters a day to friends and fans. She also answered many of Andy's letters for him. He said he avoided writing them because they gave him a headache. Writing letters was too much like real writing. The doctor told him his dizziness was caused by an inner ear problem, but Andy was sure it was because he was unable to write anything important.

— 15 —

THE TRUMPET
OF THE SWAN

For some time Andy had been working on a new children's book. This time he was writing about a trumpeter swan. He sent a letter to his old friend Cush, who lived in Philadelphia, saying that one of his characters had "the rotten nerve to take me to Philly" and, since he was not well enough to travel there, would Cush please do him a favor. Would he please go out to the zoo and take notes and snap photos of the swans there, since he had never seen a trumpeter himself. He cautioned Cush not to say a word to anyone about what he was doing because he liked to keep his projects secret. Normally he would not write about something he was not familiar with, but Louis, the trumpeter swan, insisted on having his story told.

Andy may not have known about swans, but he did have experience with many other kinds of birds. His most vivid memory was from Camp Otter of the loon mother trying to protect her tiny chick. He began to relive those memories from camp and from Augusts on Belgrade Lakes when he was a boy. In his story he creates a questioning young boy, Sam Beaver, who sets out to explore the woods and the lake. Sam needs to be alone with his thoughts so that he can figure out what he is going to be when he grows up. And he needs to keep it secret when he finds the nesting trumpeter swan.

Louis, the swan who is born without a voice, must find a way to communicate. His story becomes an adventure, almost a mystery. Will Louis be able to pay for his father's crime? Will he learn to play the trumpet? Will he find Serena and will she love him?

Andy challenges readers and teaches them many things about swans: that it takes thirty-five days for a swan to hatch; that a father swan is a cob, and a baby, a cygnet; that everyone doesn't have to like birds or even pistachio ice cream; that Louis has a dream and it's very special to follow a dream.

In fact, when the book ends we don't have answers to all of Sam's questions, especially the last one. We must go to the dictionary and look up the word *crepuscular* because White is not going to tell us that it means the glimmering light of twilight.

By Thanksgiving 1969 White had finished *The Trumpet of the Swan*. This time he sent the manuscript right off to his editor rather than putting it away for a while. He regretted that later, but said he was afraid to wait. He might not live long enough to do more. If he was going to die, he wanted to provide for Katharine. It was a familiar story.

Garth Williams did not do the illustrations this time because he had been unable to meet the publisher's deadline. White was sorry because he felt that Williams had captured his other characters perfectly, and he had enjoyed working with him. Instead, another artist was chosen to illustrate *Trumpet*. This artist depicts the gracefulness of the swans and almost makes the music ring out from Louis's trumpet. Most readers accept Louis's playing the instrument, just as they accepted Charlotte's spinning words in her web.

Andy felt Cush had helped him a great deal with his research and when the book was published he sent the first copy to his old friend with many thanks. They had a long history of shared adventures and this was one more to add to the list.

Trumpet became a best-seller immediately and moved to first place on the *New York Times* list of children's books, pushing *Charlotte's Web* to second place. Mail began pouring in. One classroom of students wrote to him saying they thought the book was more violent than his two earlier books and that they didn't believe a swan really would be able to play a trumpet.

White responded that he didn't agree, that he felt the book was for older children, at least fourth or fifth graders, who would be able to understand the old cob's actions in breaking into the music store. He explained, "I wanted a Trumpeter Swan who could play like Louis Armstrong, and I simply created him and named him Louis."

He told the students that *Trumpet* was a love story; *Charlotte*, the story of "friendship, life, death, salvation"; and *Stuart*, the "quest for beauty." White ended his letter by saying, "I think it was Jane Austen who said there were only two things in the world worth writing about—love and money. Louis had both problems. I offer no apology."

A few years later the Philadelphia Orchestra decided to perform White's story for a children's concert. He wrote a scenario that was put to music, and when he was invited to attend the performance, he said he couldn't do that unless he was asked to play in the orchestra. They called his bluff and invited him to play the triangle. But he managed to wriggle out of this invitation, as he had wriggled out of most others.

He wrote to a friend, expressing his pleasure: "Imagine me, sitting down there in my boathouse a year and a half ago, composing the lines of Sam Beaver's poem and not having the slightest inkling that the Philadelphia Orchestra was tuning up onstage. What a life I lead! How merry! How innocent! How nutty!"

When the Philadelphia City Zoo put up a sign announcing the spot where Louis and Serena had courted, Andy was very pleased to hear about it.

In 1970 Andy received the Laura Ingalls Wilder Award for his books. He could not be in Detroit to accept the award, but sent an acceptance speech, telling the group he had stumbled into writing for children, but had very definite ideas about the way he wanted to write for them. He planned never to kid them about anything and always to show them how he loved life and the world.

Again he was asked to make a new revision of the Strunk guide and kept putting it off. Once he began, he found it as difficult as it had been the first time, and said it made him dizzy. But he worked every day, including Sundays and holidays, trying to meet a November 1971 deadline. He was also working on a screenplay of *Charlotte*.

When he wanted to escape he hopped on his old three-speed bicycle and took off down the road or he went back to work on one of his carpentry projects because he found it very satisfying to work with his hands.

Letters about the *Charlotte* film passed back and forth. He kept cautioning the filmmaker to remember the animals were animals. Wilbur should act like a pig, Templeton like a rat, and Charlotte like a spider. None of them should be made into people. When he saw the film, he was not pleased. He felt the songs interrupted the story; the fair had become overblown; and Fern's interest in Henry was emphasized more than it should have been. He felt the filmmaker had tried to make the story into a moral tale when he believed animals were amoral creatures who followed their natural instincts.

Andy was awarded the National Medal for Literature in 1971 and was supposed to attend the ceremony on December 2 at Lincoln Center, but of course he did not plan to be there. Instead he found a friend who would accept the award for him. He also did not plan to attend Cornell's fiftieth reunion but told Cush that they should plan a trip together in the spring, when he expected to deliver another batch of his papers to the university. For some time he had been donating his rough drafts from the *New Yorker* columns, from his other articles, and from his children's books. He was able to deduct them from his taxes and help his alma mater at the same time.

In 1972 his goddaughter, Dorothy Lobrano Guth, asked him to consider publishing a book of his letters. Because he could never decide what to discard over the years, he had ended up saving everything. He kept his rough drafts of every

Andy interviewing a goose on his farm (Jane Lightfoot Beaumont)

article and book. He saved the drafts of letters he wrote. He saved every letter he received from fans, friends, and family. Every single piece of paper was packed away in boxes in the attic. He and Dorothy spent the next four years going through the mass of correspondence until they had selected the letters to be used in the book.

He was adamant that he would not allow a letter to be included in the book if it spoke badly of a living person. And he was finding it painful to tell so much about himself. He complained to his editor: "A man who publishes his letters becomes a nudist—nothing shelters him from the world's gaze except his bare skin."

Letters of E. B. White was published in November 1976,

and again many readers wrote to tell him how much they enjoyed the book. He had been deluged with mail a few years earlier when an article was published in honor of his seventieth birthday, and he had once told a librarian that he wished children would not write to him because he felt he had to answer and that took up all his time and kept him from writing anything else.

In earlier years Katharine tried to answer most of his fan mail for him, freeing him to write other things. She always apologized for her "secondhand reply" and explained that White's desk was "deep in unanswered letters so he has agreed to let me help him." But this time he decided to have a card printed so they would not have to answer each fan individually. He wrote a special poem for the greeting and signed it in red ink:

> To all who wrote to wish me well,
>   To all who like the *Letters*,
> I send this printed card of thanks.
>   (It frees me from my fetters.)
>
> I'd hoped to write a full reply
>   To each, to say "I love you."
> But I must face the sticky truth:
>   There's just too many *of* you.

Andy answered with a letter of his own when a group of students asked him how to write a book. "I'm not sure I can explain how to write a book," he told them. "First, you have to *want* to write one very much. Then, you have to know of something that you want to write about. Then, you have to begin. And, once you have started, you have to keep going. That's really all I know about how to write a book. I've written seventeen of them, and I'm almost ready to quit— but not quite."

To thank a class for their essays he sent an egg laid by his goose, Felicity. He told them she took about three months to lay an egg, and that she ended up with about forty eggs each spring and that each one was perfect. When they hatch, "The young are green as grass," he wrote, "and they immediately begin playing their flutes, an enchanting sound."

Eggs had been fascinating to him since he was tiny and first observed the hatching of chicks in his own backyard. No matter how old he became, or how many years he raised chickens and geese, he would never get over the miracle of the hatching egg.

He advised a young woman who was discouraged because she wanted to become a writer and didn't know how. "If you like to write and want to write, you write, no matter where you are or what else you are doing. . . ." He suggested she write something and send it to the *New Yorker* because that was what he had done over forty years before.

16

ON THE
ROPE SWING

Katharine was not well on their forty-sixth anniversary in 1975. She had been hospitalized for congestive heart failure and Andy sent her a note, telling her he had thought a great deal about a gift she might like and decided the best gift would be to build her a greenhouse, rather than to find her another piece of jewelry. Katharine was delighted with her gift, made a quick recovery, and was home to supervise the construction.

Nurses were added to their staff of cook, housekeeper, and secretary to help Katharine with her personal care. She moved slowly now, using a walker. Her voice was growing softer, and her eyes were failing. Andy's own health was a concern also. When he developed a frog in his throat he was sure it was cancer of the larynx. His hay fever still bothered his nose and eyes and made his head feel stuffy. He had never outgrown that. Now he also had high blood pressure to worry about.

Through all their illnesses White remained the devoted husband. "I don't know what I ever did to deserve a wife with Katharine's qualities," he often said, "but I have always had a lot of luck, and she was the most notable example." For him, she would always remain the beautiful, vital young woman he had married. In his eyes she did not change as the medications added to her weight and the illnesses made her grow impatient.

On the morning of July 20, 1977, Katharine told Andy she felt very sick. She had a high fever and was having trouble breathing. Once again the ambulance rushed her to the hospital. Andy sat by her bed all day, hoping she would be able to fight back the way she always had. But this time her strength was gone. He could do little but sit there, holding her hand and watching the pulsing of her heart on nearby monitors. Gradually her heart slowed and stopped and he knew Katharine was gone. Kissing her good-bye, he went back home to prepare a service for his dear K.

Andy was too upset to attend the funeral, but he asked his stepson, Roger Angell, to conduct the service and read "Lady Before Breakfast, the poem he had written for a young, vigorous Katharine. Every day he took flowers to her grave, and later he planted an oak tree there.

White stayed in the house, did his chores, and with the help of a secretary, wrote answers to the hundreds of condolence letters sent by friends and strangers who had heard about Katharine's death. He was very lonely without her, but he had to get all her papers in order and arrange all her belongings to be distributed to the family and friends she had named in her will.

After her death, Andy kept expecting to find her in the house. "When I'm upstairs, it's easy to believe K's somewhere down there," he lamented. "When I'm downstairs, I'm lulled into thinking she is up in her bedroom." The first Halloween without Katharine, Andy forced himself to greet the many children who came to his door and to comment on their costumes and disguises. His cook had made cookies for him to give the trick-or-treaters, along with apples, doughnuts, and candies. He was trying to stay interested in life, and even accepted an occasional invitation to have dinner with friends.

As a tribute to Katharine, Andy decided to put her garden articles together into a book, *Onward and Upward in the Garden*, which was published in 1979. In the introduction to the book, he described how Katharine prepared for the planting of spring bulbs. Most of the time she gardened in whatever clothing she was wearing that day. "She simply refused to dress *down* to a garden," he said. "She would kneel in the dirt and begin grubbing about, garbed in a spotless cotton dress or a handsome tweed skirt and jacket."

But on bulb day in the fall, she put on an old raincoat, overshoes, and a wool hat. Well prepared for the damp, cold weather, she brought her diagram and supervised as her helper, Henry Allen, turned the ground and planted the many bulbs she envisioned for the spring garden. Katharine's flowers continued to bring Andy pleasure after her death, and he was thrilled to see her book receiving praise. It became a great favorite, not just of gardening enthusiasts, but of the many readers who were fond of both Whites and wanted to stay in touch with them.

Andy avoided praise for his own work. When he received the *Boston Globe* award for his book of letters, he refused to attend the dinner. "I could not bear to sit around and listen to people making speeches about me or praising my books." Receiving a special Pulitzer Prize in April 1978 for "many years and many kinds of writing" was a great honor, but again he minimized its importance.

His editor on the book of letters, Corona Machemer, had suggested Andy go through his previous, unpublished writing and put together a new book. To select the pieces that would go into the book, he and Corona traveled down to Florida with many cartons of his work. They sat at a round table and tossed things into boxes labeled Yes, No, and Maybe. For a long while they kept tossing things into the No box. Nothing found its way into the Yes box.

Andy worried that he was not a real poet. In fact he called himself "a non-poet who occasionally breaks into song"; but Corona was not worried. "We will scatter the poems around in the text," she said. "We'll conceal the poems in the un-derbrush." That seemed to take care of everything and finally some stories and verses flew into the Yes box until there were enough to make a book, *Poems and Sketches*.

In 1981 he and Corona decided to celebrate their mutual birthdays by canoeing in a borrowed boat on Great Pond near where she had grown up and he had come with his family as a young boy. After that, Andy bought a canoe to use the following year. In 1983 they again celebrated their birthdays together. Andy gave Corona a Panama hat. She brought him a six-pack of Moxie, which was still being sold in Maine.

Corona also wanted Andy to publish his journals, but over the years he kept threatening to burn them. He still had not done so because he discovered that once in a while they "manage to report something in exquisite honesty and accuracy." His journals reveal the boy and the young man he had been, searching to understand himself and his place in the world. Here is the shy young man, the lonely college student, the fearful public speaker, the insecure writer.

The pages of his journal also reveal his changing dreams. Where once he had been happy raising pigeons and writing stories for *St. Nicholas*, his world expanded as he grew up. It was no longer enough to write for himself. He wanted to become a fine writer and reach a wide audience. He didn't like to talk about this dream. Instead he described Stuart's dreams, and Wilbur's, and Louis's. He made his dreams into symbols in stories, such as "The Second Tree from the Corner," but he would not describe those dreams to interviewers.

He often grew discouraged about his writing, never feeling it was good enough. He kept saying he wanted to write important and original work and complained when he had to meet deadlines in magazines because they kept him from doing so. But he certainly was not a hack, only writing for deadlines and paychecks. His work touched on his concerns for the world and the truths that most people feel.

He said what he thought about important issues and about his daily life, and readers cared. They still do. When a new book of his *New Yorker* writings was published in 1990, his fans raced to read it. They still find his essays and letters insightful and enjoyable.

He could not imagine the impact his children's stories would have. *Charlotte's Web* continues to be the book children love and choose as their favorite every year. Not far behind are *Stuart Little* and *The Trumpet of the Swan*. His poetry reflects his love of the world and the creatures in it. His adult essays are clear as a bell and still ring with emotion. Maybe his dreams have been fulfilled beyond his own expectations.

In his mid-eighties Andy was beginning to slow down and sometimes he wrote to friends about all the things he could no longer do. He had to give up skating. He had to give up his pigs, sheep, and geese, but he brought home a new puppy to make sure he would not get bored. After fifty-five years he had to give up writing newsbreaks for the magazine because his eyes were so weak.

He even joked about wanting to be eighty again because then he had been fit and could still bike and canoe and take care of all the farm chores. But he could not turn back the clock. Now he had to rely on helpers to get out his mail, keep the farm running, the house neat, and serve his meals.

The last year of his life was a difficult one, as his body and his eyes grew even weaker. He was forced to rest a great deal, until he was totally bedridden. Every day after work, Joel left his boatyard and went to visit his dad. Sometimes they talked about the past, but often Joel read to Andy, not from Thoreau's *Walden* or any of Thurber's books. Andy wanted to hear his own work. After Joel finished reading a short story or an essay or a column from the *New Yorker*, Andy had comments to make about what he had written. Sometimes he exclaimed with fervor, "That was all right."

Andy standing in front of the barn, 1962 (Stan Waterman)

Sometimes he didn't think the writing was good enough. During that year, Joel was able to read aloud and enjoy with him almost everything his dad had written. And Andy evaluated each piece, his standards just as tough as they had always been.

E. B. White died in October 1985, at the age of eighty-six. A memorial service was held on October 26, at Blue Hill Congregational Church. His stepson Roger reminded the large group of family and friends who had come that Andy would not have attended the service if he could have avoided it. Through their tears, everyone was able to find humor in that. Andy would have liked their laughter. He would have appreciated his stepdaughter's loving memories of their relationship.

He also would have liked the program his family created for that day. On one page is the poem "Natural History," written for Katharine right after their marriage with its sturdy line to connect them in life and death. On the other page is a photo of Andy swinging on the rope swing in his barn, just as Fern loves to do. On the back cover is a tiny wild iris flag to remind us of Andy's ceaseless concern for the world.

NOTES

page CHAPTER 1   A LUCKY MAN

1 "very lucky . . . children. . . ." draft letter, 7 February 1970, E. B. White Collection, Cornell University Library, Ithaca, New York.

3 "so plain . . . literature." Roger Angell, "E. B. White," *New Yorker*, 14 October 1985, 33.

On White's Maine farm, there were vegetable and flower gardens, a barn, and pasture, but if you kept walking, you came to the sea. That's why he called it a saltwater farm.

"hard work . . . sailing." E. B. White, *Letters of E. B. White*, edited by Dorothy Lobrano Guth (New York: Harper and Row, 1976), 582.

CHAPTER 2   MOUNT VERNON BOYHOOD

5 "suffered tortures . . . year," White, *Letters*, 8.

13 "met me . . . himself." Scott Elledge, *E. B. White: A Biography* (New York: W. W. Norton and Company, 1984), 18.

CHAPTER 3   GROWING UP

15 "All the . . . enjoy." E. B. White, "A Winter Walk," *St. Nicholas Magazine,* June 1911, 757.

21   "winter twilights, . . . skates. . . ." E. B. White, *One Man's Meat* (New York: Harper and Row, 1981), 88.

22   "I am . . . drafted." White, *One Man's Meat,* 89.

CHAPTER 4   CORNELL

24   "I've been . . . health." White, *One Man's Meat,* 90.

25   "small town stuff." Elledge, 52.

27   "didn't know . . . write." White, *Letters,* 510.

28   "Sergeant Strunk . . . platoon." Elledge, 55.

CHAPTER 5   GOING WEST

29   White's parents, Samuel and Jessie, moved from Summit Avenue to a smaller home on Mersereau Avenue when Elwyn was in high school.

30   "excitement of . . . enshrined" "the pure . . . glory." TL draft, 12 January 1983, E. B. White Collection.

31   "I did . . . graduated." White, *Letters,* 510.

32   "I suppose . . . promiscuously." White, *Letters,* 36–37.

33   "jogging leisurely . . . little. . . ." White, *Letters,* 39.

34   "A young . . . denotes," *E. B. White: Writings from the New Yorker 1927–1976,* edited by Rebecca Dale (New York: HarperCollins, 1990), 227.

36   "warm and . . . imagination" Elledge, 79.

    "leaned over . . . men." "skipper (who) . . . car." E. B. White, *The Second Tree from the Corner* (New York: Harper and Brothers, 1954), 39.

37   The whole episode of Hotspur on the ferry became a story, "Farewell My Lovely," which students find in their texts as an example of excellent writing.

CHAPTER 6   SEATTLE

40   "Just say . . . words," White, *Second Tree*, 12.

41   "Goodness! How . . . waitress?" E. B. White, "Years of Wonder," *Essays of E. B. White* (New York: Harper and Row, 1977), 179.

42   "I reeled . . . followed." E. B. White, *The Points of My Compass* (New York: Harper and Row, 1962), 239.

CHAPTER 7   THE *NEW YORKER*

46   "the world . . . misfortunes." Elledge, 107.

49   "Lost—Male . . . nasturtiums." E. B. White, *Ho Hum: Newsbreaks from "The New Yorker"* (New York: Farrar and Rinehart, 1931), 60.

50   "Finally he . . . inclined." E. B. White, *Another Ho Hum: More Newbreaks from "The New Yorker"* (New York: Farrar and Rinehart, 1932), 82.

CHAPTER 8   MARRIAGE

56   "The spider, . . . returning." E. B. White, *Poems and Sketches of E. B. White* (New York: Harper and Row, 1981), 72.

59   "the nursery . . . neatly." White, *Letters,* 99.

      "walks now . . . thanksgiving." White, *Letters*, 109.

60   "gulls scream . . . terriers," TL draft, 13 June 1936, E. B. White Collection.

      "It looks . . . in," E. B. White, Interview by Susan Frank, 28 September 1964, E. B. White Collection.

61   "What do . . . Rivera." White, *Poems and Sketches*, 35–36.

62 "In some . . . eggs." E. B. White, *Every Day Is Saturday* (New York: Harper and Brothers, 1934) 182.

"It's almost . . . letters." Linda Davis, *Onward and Upward: A Biography of Katharine S. White* (New York: Harper and Row, 1987), 115.

64 "he had . . . anyway." Davis, 122.

"I have . . . cord." White, *Letters,* 170.

"You may . . . writer." Elledge, 205.

CHAPTER 9   MOVE TO MAINE
67 "shingling a . . . idea." White, *Letters,* 180.

"I would . . . else." White, *Letters*, 157.

68 "Just like lightning." White, *One Man's Meat,* 44.

"after-dinner mint" White, *One Man's Meat,* 187.

70 "our finest . . . one." Elledge, 228.

71 "mice in . . . spine." Elledge, 251.

CHAPTER 10   *STUART LITTLE*
73 "I would . . . children." White, *Letters,* 194.

75 "children can . . . make-believe." Elledge, 265.

"second son." E. B. White, *Stuart Little* (New York: Harper and Row, 1973), 1.

"fresh smell . . . day." White, *Stuart Little,* 13.

"breeze in . . . overhead. . . ." White, *Stuart Little,* 31.

"A shaft . . . tidy," White, *Stuart Little,* 92.

78 "with a . . . bosom," White, *Stuart Little,* 128.

79 "Original Work." White, *Letters,* 205.

CHAPTER II   NEW YORK AGAIN

82   "In it ... THINKER. ..." White, *Letters,* 277.

83   "a blank ... it.' " White, *Letters,* 280.

84   "I can ... cat." White, *Letters,* 285.

85   "If I ... America." White, *Letters,* 286.

"continue to ... man. ..." White, *Letters,* 287.

"expects every ... pie." James Thurber, "E. B. W." *Saturday Review of Literature,* 15 October 1938, 8–9.

86   "filled up ... apprehension." White, *Letters,* 294.

"emptiness ... and vapors." White, *Letters*, 295.

87   "He wanted ... fair." White, *Writings*, 232.

CHAPTER I2   *CHARLOTTE'S WEB*

91   "to ripen." Elledge, 295.

"Charlotte was ... Wilbur." Folders A–I, E. B. White Collection.

"A barn ... about." Folders A–I, E. B. White Collection.

"Where's Papa ... ax?" Folders A–I, E. B. White Collection.

92   "It is ... both." Folders A–I, E. B. White Collection.

"It is ... perfect." Eudora Welty, *The Eye of the Story* (New York: Vintage Books, 1979), 205.

"the most ... book." Elledge, 298.

93   "Children are ... time" E. B. White, Interview, in *Writers at Work: The Paris Review Interviews,* 8th series, edited by George Plimpton (New York: Penguin Books, 1988), 20.

CHAPTER I3   THOREAU'S INFLUENCE

95   "I keep ... despair." Elledge, 313.

96 "if one . . . success. . . ." White, *Points,* 17.

"He was . . . century." White, *Writings,* 40.

97 "we discard . . . out." White, *Letters,* 510.

"we should . . . laundry." White, *Letters,* 510.

"To affect . . . arts." White, *Letters,* 510–511.

98 "I sound . . . write." White, *Points,* flap.

"at the . . . ahead." White, *Letters,* 415.

CHAPTER 14   MAINE, YEAR-ROUND

101 "To My . . . so." White, *Poems and Sketches,* 93.

102 "the members . . . man," White, Interview, *Paris,* 12.

103 White went through agony each week as he prepared his *New Yorker* paragraphs, according to Roger Angell. Interview with author, 9 January 1991.

104 "A man . . . window." White, *Points,* 64.

106 "They drive . . . before." White, *Writings,* 100.

"I believe . . . world." White, *Essays,* 93.

107 "It may . . . fall." White, Interview, *Paris,* 11.

108 Stan Waterman remembered seeing the Whites wearing surgical masks at his Florida lecture. Telephone interview with author, 28 January 1991.

CHAPTER 15   *THE TRUMPET OF THE SWAN*

111 "the rotten . . . Philly." White, *Letters,* 567.

113 "I wanted . . . Louis." White, *Letters,* 644.

"friendship, life . . . beauty." White, *Letters,* 645.

"I think . . . apology." White, *Letters*, 645.

114   Allene White said that Andy wiggled out of every invitation he could. Telephone interview with author, 18 September 1990.

"Imagine me, . . . nutty!" White, *Letters,* 612.

116   "A man . . . skin." White, *Letters*, 655.

117   "secondhand reply . . . him." Davis, xi.

"To all . . . you." E. B. White Collection.

"I'm not . . . quite." White, *Letters,* 571.

118   "The young . . . sound." White, *Letters*, 553.

"If you . . . doing. . . ." White, *Letters*, 649.

CHAPTER 16   ON THE ROPE SWING

120   "I don't . . . example." Elledge, 354.

121   "When I'm . . . bedroom." Isabel Russell, *Katharine and E. B. White: An Affectionate Memoir* (New York: W. W. Norton, 1988), 196.

"She simply . . . jacket." Davis, xviii.

122   "I could . . . books." Russell, 228.

"many years . . . writing," E. B. White Collection.

"a non-poet . . . song" White, *Poems and Sketches,* xiii.

"We will . . . underbrush," White, *Poems and Sketches,* xv.

123   "manage to . . . accuracy." White, Interview, *Paris,* 22.

124   Joel White described how close he became to his dad that last year. Interview with author, 17 September 1990.

"That was all right." Roger Angell, Interview with author, 9 January 1991.

BIBLIOGRAPHY

ANGELL, ROGER. "E. B. White." Talk of the Town. *New Yorker,* 14 October 1985, 31.

———. Interview with author, 9 January 1991.

BRADBURY, PATRICIA. "What a Life Otter Bee." *Cottage Life,* June 1989.

DAVIS, LINDA. *Onward and Upward: A Biography of Katharine S. White.* New York: Harper and Row, 1987.

EDMAN, IRWIN. "E. B. White, That Fine Goldsmith in Words." *New York Herald Tribune Weekly Book Review,* 10 November 1946.

ELLEDGE, SCOTT. *E. B. White: A Biography.* New York: W. W. Norton and Company, 1984.

FRANK, SUSAN. "E. B. White Recalls Cornell Years." *Cornell Daily Sun,* 10 October 1964.

GILL, BRENDAN. *Here at the New Yorker.* New York: Random House, 1975.

NEUMEYER, PETER F. "The Creation of *Charlotte's Web,*" Part I and Part II. *Horn Book,* October and December 1982, 489, 617.

———. "*Stuart Little*: The Manuscripts by Peter Neumeyer." *Horn Book,* September/October 1988, 593.

RUSSELL, ISABEL. *Katharine and E. B. White: An Affectionate Memoir.* New York: W. W. Norton, 1988.

SAMPSON, EDWARD C. *E. B. White.* New York: Twayne Publications, 1974.

STRUNK, WILLIAM, JR., AND E. B. WHITE. *The Elements of Style, 3d ed.* New York: Macmillan, 1979.

THURBER, JAMES. "E. B. W." *Saturday Review of Literature,* 15 October 1938.

THURBER, JAMES, AND E. B. WHITE. *Is Sex Necessary? or, Why You Feel the Way You Do.* New York: Harper and Row, 1984.

WELTY, EUDORA. *The Eye of the Story.* New York: Vintage Books, 1979.

WHITE, ALLENE. Telephone interview with author, 18 September 1990.

White, E. B. *Another Ho Hum: More Newsbreaks from "The New Yorker."* New York: Farrar and Rinehart, 1932.

———. *Charlotte's Web.* New York: Harper and Row, 1973.

———. The E. B. White Collection. Department of Rare Books, Cornell University Library, Ithaca, New York.

———. *An E. B. White Reader.* Edited by William W. Watt and Robert W. Bradford. New York: Harper and Row, 1977.

———. *E. B. White: Writings from the New Yorker 1927–1976.* Edited by Rebecca Dale. New Yorker: HarperCollins, 1990.

———. *Essays of E. B. White.* New York: Harper and Row, 1977.

———. *Every Day Is Saturday.* New York: Harper and Brothers, 1934.

———. *Here Is New York.* New York: Curtis Publishing Company, 1949.

———. *Ho Hum: Newsbreaks from "The New Yorker."* New York: Farrar and Rinehart, 1931.

———. Interview by Susan Frank, 28 September 1964. Tape recording.

———. Interview. In *Writers at Work: The Paris Review Interviews,* 8th series. Edited by George Plimpton. New York: Penguin Books, 1988.

———. *Letters of E. B. White.* Edited by Dorothy Lobrano Guth. New York: Harper and Row, 1976.

———. *One Man's Meat.* New York: Harper and Row, 1981.

———. *Poems and Sketches of E. B. White.* New York: Harper and Row, 1981.

———. *The Points of My Compass.* New York: Harper and Row, 1962.

———. *Quo Vadimus.* New York: Garden City Publishing Company, 1946.

———. *The Second Tree from the Corner.* New York: Harper and Brothers, 1954.

———. *Stuart Little.* New York: Harper and Row, 1973.

———. *The Trumpet of the Swan.* New York: Harper and Row, 1970.

———. "A Winter Walk." *St. Nicholas Magazine,* June 1911, 757.

WHITE, JOEL. Interview with author, 17 September 1990.

WHITE, KATHARINE S. *Onward and Upward in the Garden.* New York: Farrar, Straus, and Giroux, 1979.

INDEX